Eddie Paul's
Custom
Bodywork
Handbook

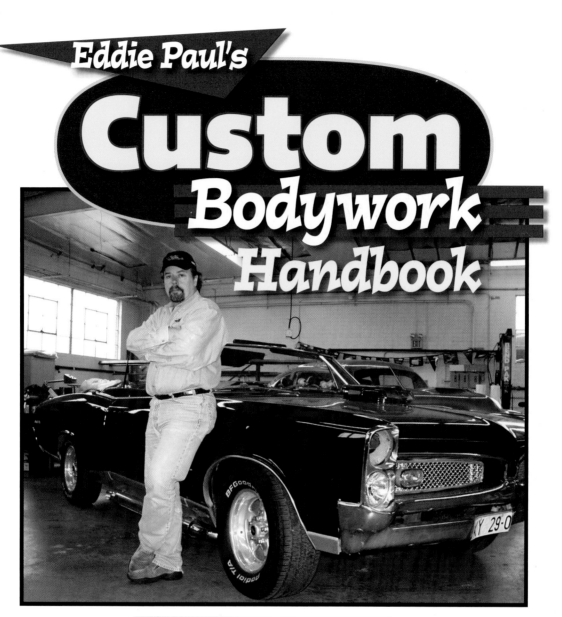

Published by

kp books
An Imprint of F+W Publications

700 East State Street • Iola, WI 54990-0001
715-445-2214 • 888-457-2873

Our toll-free number to place an order or obtain
a free catalog is (800) 258-0929.

Library of Congress Catalog Number Applied For
ISBN: 0-89689-232-8

Designed by Jon Stein
Edited by Brian Earnest
Printed in the United States of America

Dedication

To God, for allowing me to live through what I have lived through, and my wife Renee, for tolerating my eccentricities and inspiring me onward as well as all the time she puts in keeping us financially afloat, and Ariel for making Renee and I laugh along the way as she learns a trade she may never need or want.

Special thanks

To all of the companies and their representatives (listed individually throughout the book) who provided services, materials or equipment to facilitate the various steps of customizing, and to the following individuals: Brian Hatano, my general manager; Jon Forseth my machine shop foreman; and to the rest of the E.P. Industries crew (Bruce, Peggy, Jeff, Mario, Dave, Rich, Jose and Al) for the support as well as the ulcers.

Contents

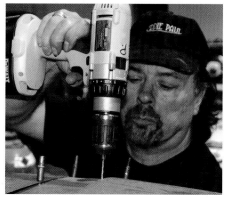

By Jay Leno

I met Eddie Paul through a mutual contact at Snap-On Tools so I knew we had at least one thing in common right from the start. As a "car guy," I love to meet other car guys, and Eddie falls into that category at the top of the list.

It's not often that a guy can go to a shop today and see the type of customizing that started hot rodding back in the '50s and '60s. Those were the years when I became familiar with names like Winfield, Roth, and Starbird, and the cars that they built helped to build my enthusiasm for high-performance and customizing. The names, as well as the cars, have evolved over the years and there's a whole new breed of customizers making themselves known. At the forefront is Eddie Paul, an experienced customizer who started back in those formative hot rodding years who combines traditional hot rodding with new technology.

When I walk through Eddie's shop, I'm totally blown away by all the outrageous vehicles being built. When you read this book, you'll get an over-the-shoulder look at how he does it all. While having Eddie's shop lay a custom pearl blue paint job on my new 502-cubic-inch Boss Hoss V-8 motorcycle, I got a preview of what goes on at Customs By Eddie Paul. Eddie's imaginative mind, sound business sense, and total enthusiasm for cars makes him the ideal person to write a book on automotive customizing. From one car guy to another, I think you'll really enjoy *Eddie Paul's Custom Bodywork Handbook*.

Introduction

OZENS OF GOOD AND NOT-SO-GOOD BOOKS have been written on the subject of both automotive customizing and metal fabrication, but none have been written the "Eddie Paul style"…until now. Like the cars that I build, I hope you'll find that my way of putting information into book form will be entertaining. Rather than rehash the same stale information that other books do, along with the usual stuff on customizing, fabrication techniques and special tools of my trade, I've added a number of anecdotes about how I got my start in customizing, the high-profile jobs that have come my way, and the obstacles that I've had to overcome in the process of becoming "Hollywood's Best Kept Secret." I figure that maybe writing about some of the trials and tribulations of my career may help you get into (or stay out of!) the business of customizing!

I suppose that some of you may know me for the cars that I've built recently for movies like *Triple X* and *The Fast and the Furious*. But it all started what seems like an eternity ago. I guess it has been somewhat of an eternity now that I have to put it down in writing…

A few decades ago when I was 17, I had to open my first customizing shop (Customs by Eddie Paul) in the small town of El Segundo in sunny southern California. I say "had to" because my friendly small-town neighbors had grown tired of my grinding and welding at all hours of the day and night, as I rushed to finish one project after another.

The first week in my new shop was a bit scary, as I had to come up with the first and last month's rent, totaling $700 ($350 per month). But much to my surprise, and before I even realized what was happening, by the end of that first month my fledgling business had outgrown what I thought at first was a very large shop and was starting to accumulate an anxiously waiting list of customers wanting to have me build custom cars and bikes. And it wasn't that big of a

leap into the movie business from building custom cars for people and magazines.

Within a month or two of opening my new little shop, a guy stopped in and asked if I could build about 50 cars within two weeks for a movie he was working on. In my normal style of overconfidence I said "sure no problem." In response, he quietly handed me a small stack of money to start on the project, which I later found out was called *Grease* and the rest of the story is history.

Thinking back, I could have taken the money and ran off to Mexico for the vacation of my life, or, I could stay at the shop and work around the clock on a project that everyone else turned down as "impossible." I opted for the route less traveled and decided to work my butt to the bone, make the cars and hope that Hollywood would call back someday—which they did, many, many times—just to throw me another impossible task or two and hear me say "sure, no problem."

Well that was then and this is now and it has been well over 30 years that I have been building hundreds of cars for the studios. Many of my cars have been in blockbuster films. Aside from the 48 cars we built in just two weeks that were used in *Grease,* I also built many of the cars used in the first season of *The Dukes of Hazzard*, and was the first person to build the pipe ramp used in thousands of movies, since the first one I built for stuntman Gary Baxley on the *Dukes.*

There were a pair of convertible 1950 Mercs (two identical Mercs, one for stunts, the other for backup and close-ups) for the movie *Streets of Fire* along with the Studebaker police cars in the film, and the four chopped-top 1950 Mercs for the film *Cobra*. We built all of them, as well as the 70-plus bikes used in *The Streets of Fire*. For *Mask*, I built the bikes and cars as well as coordinated the stunts for the actors and bikers, then life became a real blur

Eddie with the spectacular *xXx* GTO.

with hundred of cars for MTV, commercials and TV as well as promotional vehicles for companies such as McDonalds and many others. For the film "The Fast and the Furious" my shop built about 80 cars in one month. For the *xXx* movie, we were hired to make the seven versions of the GTO as well as the rest of the stunt cars used throughout various scenes. This consumed about five weeks of our time. We then built the 200-plus cars for *2Fast 2Furious* within a span of two months. A week after the last car left our shop, the film *Taxi* came along.

None of the movie projects we have ever done were as much of a challenge, mentally and physically, as *2Fast 2Furious*. The shear quantity of cars was staggering, the time schedule was frightening, and the pay was appalling. But the results made movie car history!

I might add that I have never met as many people trying to take credit for the cars as I have on *2Fast 2Furious*. If someone walked by the shop as we were building the cars they seem to think that they built the cars. I don't get it. If someone ever tells you that they built a car for a film, find out if they even know how to weld or fabricate; many do not, they only talk as if they do. It is sad that someone needs attention so badly that they will steal the credits from others.

For *2Fast 2Furious*, we had to have set some kind of world record for car customizing, as we churned out modified vehicles at a frightening average pace of 3.3 cars per day. Looking back, it seems like a blur, cars were coming and going faster than I could note the changes we made to them.

It wasn't until I wrote my first book "The Cars of the Fast and the Furious" that I could take the time to sit down and organize my notes on the cars. Exactly what we did to each and every car will never be totally sorted out but a fairly accurate record is, at least, now put in print.

I consider myself very blessed to have so many "hits" under my belt, but have to admit it has not been easy or cheap. It has also caused more than a few gray hairs and pushed me, as well as my wife Renee, to the brink of terror as I get her to write a check for a few dozen cars based on the word of a transportation coordinator that "I have the show."

It may be hard to believe, but I have never had a contract or any piece of paper other than a few notes as to what I should build. It has all been on a word-of-mouth agreement or a handshake, but this is between people I have known for a quite a few years and trust.

If I waited for a contract from the studios, it would be too late to build the cars. You see, I don't get the movie cars because I am the lowest bidder; I get them because I get the job done on time, and this is more important than anything. Who cares how they look if they are late? Or who cares how cheap they are if they do not make it to the set on time? The biggest attribute we can have when we take on a job is that, no matter what they throw at us, it is finished when we say it will be, and many times earlier by mere minutes. I have taken on as many as five movies at one time and finished all on time. It was not easy, but we did it! Many times I hang up the phone from a "deal" and start buying cars within minutes of the verbal phone deal.

Utilizing the many years of film work I decided that the focus of this book is a little different than my first book. That book was a general overall coverage of the exact cars

This is a *Fast and Furious* style car that we built for one of the guys in the shop as well as the *Motor Trend* car show circuit. It's a good example of a tuner-style custom.

Two car guys: Eddie and Jay.

You may remember the Supra used in both *The Fast and the Furious* (orange then) and *2Fast 2Furious* (gold now). We put that car together in about four days. Most of the stuff was just a bolt-on kit. The hardest part was the paint.

This is another example of a tuner I built for myself. It shows that sometimes just a fancy color scheme can really make a car stand out from the crowd. This car has a body kit and tinted windows. Ape Wraps did the vinyl application at our shop in just than a few hours.

we built for a film. This book is a step-by-step guide to "customizing" with "inside tips and tricks" you could only learn by working at my shop or building a unique custom car for yourself.

Most of the work performed on cars is not that hard to do if broken down into simple steps which, if you know how to break the job down, almost anyone can do. Hopefully, you will gain skill, knowledge and confidence as you progress from one project to the next.

By the end of this book, if you follow what I recommend, you will have a pretty substantial collection of tools to start a career in "customizing" as well as the knowledge of how to use them in the construction of a custom car, truck or bike.

I have been to hundreds of production meeting at a major studios as we talked about the different cars I was going to build for them, and I have been asked more than once, "Now you have built one of these before… haven't you?" Once, this question came in reference to the 60-foot-long, eight-wheeled "Battlecraft" used in the feature film *Ice Pirates*. And I would look the producer in the eyes intently and in a matter-of-fact attitude just say "no." Then after what seems like hours of silence, the producer would laugh and tell everyone in the room "sure he has… he is only joking." And the meeting would go on; I would get the job and deliver the Battlecraft on schedule. Later, to be approached by the same producer telling me "you really had me worried, I thought you were serious about not having built one of these." I found it better to just smile and not answer than to get into it with him. The point of this story is that, like in the book *Catch 22*, many people think you cannot do something unless you have done

it before. I prefer to think if you have never done it before, you can do it, you just have to learn about it, start on it and do it. Most people never start, out of fear of failure.

Almost all custom work can be boiled down to a simple formula; concept, research, design, layout, and application. It doesn't matter if it is a square box or an exotic car; it just requires knowledge of materials and a skill of how to work with them. The skill will come with time. I have found that building things is a lot like music: If you know how to play any instrument, it is not that hard to learn to play a different instrument. You already are armed with the basic knowledge, as well as the confidence that you can do it.

I recently was lucky enough to be invited to Jay Leno's garage to see all of his cars and motorcycles and the most interesting part of the tour, for me, was his shop where his four employees build and restore his cars. Just the shop alone revealed a lot about the skill level of his guys. There was not a lot of fancy shiny new tools, but old and used tools, many dating back to the '40s and '50s, showing that you do not always need new tools or a lot of tools, but you need to know how to use what tools you have. His guys could make almost anything out of his shop. They have the skill many people only wish they had. The cars were great and very rare, but the tools really got my attention. I could spend hours just looking at all of them. In fact, later, Jay sent a mechanical stretcher over for me to repair and it was just fun working on such a well-made machine. I think it could have been older than me, and it now works great.

But enough about me, let's get into some customizing!

Chapter One

Metalworking 101—Fundamentals of Fabrication

Metal Selection, Gauge, Size and Composition

Customizing is all about working with metal. Aluminum, alloys, mild steel, cold-rolled, hot-rolled, sheet, bar stock, tubing… Before you begin to fabricate anything, you have to know your metals. And once you know your metals, you must know how to work with them. Did you know there are more than 26 different types of aluminum alloys alone? Each and every one has unique properties, some of which are different enough that they cannot be welded together or may break when subjected to a particular force. For this reason, any good text on customizing and fabrication needs to start with a lesson on metal.

When it comes to customizing a car, truck or motorcycle, mild steel is the type of metal most commonly used to modify or fabricate with. It can be fused directly onto a steel body or frame through welding. All other materials, including fiberglass, plastics, and aluminum, are relegated to bolt-on status; however, these materials can be attached and molded to a steel body with some degree of longevity through chemical bonding. Since most car bodies that we choose to customize are manufactured of steel, most of the modifications and technical information in this book will focus on working with steel.

Metallurgy is simply the science of metal and metal alloy. Everything from selection of the correct type of metal, composition, gauge (thickness) and size, to welding, treatments, and working techniques will be better understood with a fundamental knowledge of metallurgy. An experienced customizer can quickly determine which

We try to keep a large variety of alloys and gauges of steel and aluminum as many of our projects come in at night and we need metal when the metal yards are closed.

type of metal to fabricate a roll bar with, or what alloy to use for the aluminum panels in an engine compartment. The proceeding chapters of this book will give you some of that basic knowledge along with the techniques and tricks of the customizing trade that you'll be able to use to fabricate virtually anything.

In this chapter, we'll cover the fundamentals of metal. The basics, rather than the heavy science of metallurgy, is all you need to know in order to become proficient at automotive customizing. Once you become familiar with the different alloys, some recommendations for their application, and the best ways to work with them, you will find that you can concentrate on the specific type of metal and the techniques that will help your project along.

Try to keep the steel and aluminum separated because they can contaminate each other and lead to problems during welding.

Tubing and bar is another hard item to keep around the shop and our steel racks and aluminum racks are never fully stocked.

We use all type alloys and gauges of metal on our projects, such as the door frame extension of a top chop we were working on. It had to match the gauge of the existing car, so we used an AK steel of 18 gauge.

You'll also be able to determine exactly what to maintain in your supply of metals so that you'll conveniently have that special alloy when it comes time to fabricate that special part.

The two types of metal that you'll be working with most frequently in automotive customizing are steel (mild and, to a lesser degree, stainless), and aluminum. The difference between the various types of steel and aluminum are from the extra ingredients, or alloys, which essentially are other types of metal blended together with the base metal to enhance one or more aspects, such as strength, corrosion resistance, ductility or malleability. The weldability of metal can also be changed just by adding a percentage of one or more metals, so the first thing to remember is that a metal's alloy content is an important factor to consider during the working stages of metal as well as for the structural integrity of its application.

At Customs By Eddie Paul, we often use 3003-H14 aluminum alloy (refer to the alloy definitions below) for much of our fabrication. The 3003-H14 has superior strength characteristics over pure aluminum and is easily welded with either TIG (tungsten-inert-gas) or oxygen-acetylene gas welders, yet remains malleable for shaping and bending. By comparison, a 6061-T6 aluminum alloy would yield even more strength than the 3003-H14, but the 6061-T6 is also more brittle and if welded, may develop stress cracks at the weld.

Following is a list of aluminum alloys defined by a four-digit numeric code to identify the alloy content. The first digit represents the main element of the alloy. The alphanumeric code that follows the four digits (i.e "H14" or "T6") is the hardness and temper specification of an alloy. For example, a letter "F" in the temper code refers to *fabricated*, which is an aluminum that has not been treated for hardness. A letter "O" indicates *annealed*, or softened by a process of heating and cooling. A letter "H" indicates a *strain-hardened* alloy (hardened by cold-working), and a letter "T" means *heat-treated*. Generally speaking, the higher the number in the temper code, the harder and stronger the alloy.

1XXX (1000-series) is the designation for unalloyed (99 percent pure) aluminum. The 1000-series offers high corrosion resistance, excellent workability and welds easily; however, its low strength limits its use in certain applications. This is still a common alloy for use in automotive fabrication where strength is not an issue. Non-heat-treatable.

This is the inside trunk of the 1950 Merc we built for the movie *Cobra*. The aluminum was a 3000 series and toward the soft end of the heat treat scale so it could be cut and formed with ease.

A panel can be patched so well that you cannot see the patch, but the gauge and alloy are important for the end results.

2XXX (2000-series) is an aluminum containing copper as its main alloy. 2000-series aluminum alloy provides a better strength-to-weight ratio than 1000-series and is also easy to work with. The trade-off, though, is that this alloy is not as ductile, meaning that bend radii must be fairly large and gradual, and joining pieces of 2000-series alloy must be accomplished by riveting or chemical bonding rather than welding. Heat-treatable.

3XXX (3000-series) indicates an aluminum with a main alloy of manganese. The addition of manganese yields a 20-percent increase in strength over 1000-series, yet it retains the working qualities of pure aluminum, and can be TIG or gas welded. For these reasons, 3000-series aluminum alloy is the most popular choice among automotive fabricators. Non-heat-treatable.

4XXX (4000-series) is an aluminum alloyed with silicon. Moderate strength.

5XXX (5000-series) is an aluminum alloyed with magnesium. Moderate-to-high strength. Non-heat-treatable.

6XXX (6000-series) such as 6061-T4 or 6061-T6 is commonly used in production due to its relatively low cost and excellent mechanical properties. Annealed 6000-series aluminum alloy (or 6000-series with an "O" temper code) also lends itself to forming. Heat-treatable.

7XXX (7000-series) is an aluminum alloyed with zinc. 7000-series offers the greatest strength, but is the least ductile. Heat-treatable.

Fortunately, the selection of steel suitable for automotive fabrication is more abbreviated than that of aluminum and therefore less confusing. Steel is an alloy of iron, of which there are two types: *carbon steel* and *alloy steel*. While some high-end customizers make liberal use of *stainless* steel, which is an alloy steel, the level of skill required to work with it is likewise at the higher end of the scale. Stainless

steel is a corrosion-resistant steel commonly alloyed with a high percentage of chromium and nickel. There are many appealing structural and cosmetic qualities associated with the use of stainless steel, however, so you may want to consider advancing your skills once you have mastered the basics.

There are some fabrication jobs that we do in my shop that require the strength and weight of steel along with the corrosion resistance of aluminum. For example, the 14-foot mechanical great white sharks that I build for the Cousteaus and The Discovery Channel specials are framed entirely out of stainless steel. With constant exposure to the harsh salt water, any part of the shark structure made of carbon steel would corrode and fail within a few short days. By the way, not all stainless steel is "stainless." Like aluminum, there are several stainless alloys with varying degrees of corrosion resistance, strength, etc.

For general automotive work, my use of stainless is usually limited to hardware items such as fasteners (bolts, nuts, washers, etc.). Occasionally, a job comes up where we fabricated portions of a frame or some brackets out of stainless. Stainless can be very easily machine-polished to a high chrome-like luster. But the cost factor for both material and labor usually keeps us working with carbon steel.

Carbon steel, a combination of iron and carbon, is used in most of the techniques in this book. But to avoid any confusion down the line, there are a few other terms that I may use in reference to steel. One is *mild* steel. Mild steel is simply a carbon steel that contains a maximum of 0.20 percent carbon. Mild steel cannot be hardened or tempered, but it can be case-hardened. *Hot-rolled* steel is a carbon steel that is brought up to a white heat during its manufacture and then passed through a series of rolls to reduce the cross section, thereby increasing its length. It is then cooled,

Sheet Metal Safety and Storage Tips

Handling sheets of metal can be one of the most dangerous jobs in the shop. My dad once cut his thumb off with a 4 x 8 sheet of 22-gauge steel just by carrying it the wrong way. It was my first lesson in safety. It happened when his friend, who was helping him carry the sheet slipped and dropped his end of it. Since they were both carrying it by the vertical edge, the heavy sheet slipped out of my dad's hand and sliced his thumb off in the process. He had it put back on (by a drunken doctor I might add; the only one he could find in the small town) but it never worked again. He told me the story so many times I thought I would pass it on, as it has taught me respect for the material. I now carry sheet metal by the top edge or with Vise Grips.

Storing sheets of metal the right way will help to avoid moving the heavy sheets unnecessarily when it's time to use them. Organize your metal by type and size; you can even label each sheet if you have to. Most garages won't afford you the space to store sheet metal properly so they end up leaning against a wall. But if you can, store them flat and at table height so you can simply slide them on to your layout table. Flat storage will keep the sheets flat, with no bends or warpage.

Regardless of whether sheet metal is stored upright or flat, the edges and corners can still pose a danger if left exposed. I often walk out in the shop and see the corner of a sheet hanging off the end of a table. I stop, shake my head, and slide it back in before I give the same boring lecture on safety to everyone in the area. That sharp corner is the same as a knife blade sticking out. Always keep your sheet of metal on the table top.

While I'm on the subject of safety, wear gloves as well as goggles when handling and cutting metal. Air nozzles, grinders, nibblers and saws will throw metal particles in all directions and leave razor-sharp edges. And the time that it takes to put on gloves and goggles is less than the time it takes to get to the emergency center to get a cut stitched up or a piece of metal pulled out of your face. (Note: In my photos, you will no doubt see me or my employees working without safety gear. We've all been cut, burned, punctured and gouged, so I speak from experience about safety equipment.)

cut to length, or coiled. *Cold-rolled* steel is a carbon steel that is manufactured by a process technically refered to as *cold reduction*. The cold-reduction process reduces, as its name implies, the thickness of steel by rolling or drawing the material without preheating it. This cold method adds strength as well as produces stock that is smoother and more consistent.

The process of hot-rolling produces a surface slag that, when compared side-by-side with cold-rolled steel, is quite obvious. The benefit to using hot-rolled is its lower cost. The more expensive cold-rolled steel is commonly used in precision sheet metal applications since it provides an excellent surface, material consistency and a more accurate thickness.

The same basic code system that defines aluminum alloys similarly defines steel. But before we get into coding, let me say that I seldom have to refer to or order my steel by code as I do with aluminum. The main reason is that I've developed a rapport with the metal supplier that I get all of my metal from and I simply refer to my carbon steel orders as either *hot-rolled* or *cold-rolled*. When it comes time for you to locate a metal supplier and place an order, keep in mind that a good supplier will have a catalog of the metal that they stock that usually contains a lot of useful information pertaining to sizes, gauges and alloys. And a knowledgeable salesman will also take the time to help

you with your order based on your specific requirements. Still, it's always good to know what you're ordering so the following code definitions are part of this portion of custom bodywork. This is not a complete list of codes; I've narrowed it down to the basics to avoid any confusion.

1XXX (1000-series): Basic open-hearth and acid Bessemer carbon steel that is non-sulfurized. 1020-series cold-rolled steel sheet metal is a common material for automotive fabrication.

2XXX (2000-series): Steel alloyed with the addition of nickel.

3XXX (3000-series): Steel alloyed with nickel and about 1.25 to 3.50 percent chromium.

4XXX (4000-series): Steel alloyed with molybdenum or nickel-chromium-molybdenum. You've probably heard the term "4130 chrome-moly" a few times. 4130 is a steel alloyed with chromium and molybdenum. Stress-relieved 4130 chrome-moly is used where structure strength is most critical. Annealed chrome-moly is used for fabricating structures that require forming and bending.

The code series for steel continues up to 9XXX (9000-series) with different alloys and percents of additional metals being added that will enhance different features and characteristics of the base carbon steel. As you get more involved in sheet metal fabrication (as opposed to

AK steel can be wheeled with relative ease and stretched or shrunk to fit an area in your car so well that it looks "factory." All it takes is time and knowledge, a few tools, some metal and lot of coffee!

This rear window patch was made from steel and shaped to match a missing roof piece within a few hours. This panel replaced the rear window on the Project 40.

fabricating with bar stock or tubing), there are specific types of steel that you can use to enhance the working properties during the forming process.

My steel preference for general all-around customizing are two alloys referred to as AK and SK steel sheet. This is the metal we use at the shop for most of our metal fabrication. I would suggest you purchase AK or SK. "A" indicating the addition of aluminum during the killing process indicated by the "K" for "Killed" or in the case of SK, the addition of silicon. The metal supplier for my shop, M&K Metal in Gardena, California, has both AK and SK steel sheet stock and will sell single and partial sheets at a time, whereas some metal suppliers will only sell these metals in mega-pound quantities.

You will find this metal to be the best all-around alloy for metal fabrication of parts and panels. You will notice that if you work AK or SK steel it will not work-harden as quickly as regular cold-rolled steel does. This is a very big advantage for the fabrication of deeply contoured panels. If you cannot find the AK or SK near you at your local metal supply company, try calling any local customizer or stamping company. Many times they have already bought a few thousand pounds of it and may be willing to sell a few sheets to a fellow fabricator. I have, on many occasions, gotten together with someone else and placed a combined order; this will render a quantity discount on most items.

I use 18-gauge AK sheet metal for most of the customizing in our shop. As a rule of thumb, I try to match the gauge of sheet metal to that of the panels on the car that I'm working on. For a stand-alone project, 18-gauge is a little heavier than necessary, but this thickness does allow for deeper shapes to be formed into the metal. Although 20-gauge would be easier to cut and shape, 18-gauge sheet is perhaps the best for a beginning fabricator to start with.

Gauge: The Thickness of Steel and Aluminum

The gauge of sheet metal is a numeric reference that indicates thickness. It's similar to the gauge scale for electrical wire in that a numerically higher gauge indicates a thinner material. This can sometimes be referred to as "the inverse law of logic as it pertains to sheet metal gauge." Whether it's sheet metal or electrical wire, this gauge system seems backwards to me, but we're stuck with it.

If you make a side-by-side comparison, the same gauge number of a sheet of steel (ferrous) and a sheet of aluminum (non-ferrous) is different in actual thickness; in other words, the two sheet materials with equal measurements in thousandths of an inch will have different gauge numbers. For example, 20-gauge steel is 0.0359-inch thick while 20-gauge aluminum is 0.0320-inch thick; not a big difference, but enough to be confusing to some of the engineers out there. So 20-gauge aluminum is closer to 21-gauge steel, which is 0.0329-inch thick. Don't ask me why, I have no idea. But it will mess you up when you are trying to match a gauge in a repair or when adding new metal, so be sure to specify the thickness, the gauge and the material when ordering your metal. Most of the material we work with in my shop is between 18 and 22 gauge.

Metal Shrinking: How To Shrink Metal and Why

So what exactly is metal *shrinking*? Well, to a fabricator, it's when you literally pull or press a section of metal together into itself. Doing this doesn't actually make any metal go away, but it reshapes it and makes that particular section of metal a bit thicker. This is one way to shape the

Metal shrinking can be accomplished in a number of ways. One of the oldest is the oxy-acetylene torch method of heating, pounding and letting the metal cool. For this type of shrinking, find the area that is too high (indicating too much metal) and simply heat it to a cherry red, moving the torch around as you heat so you do not burn through the metal.

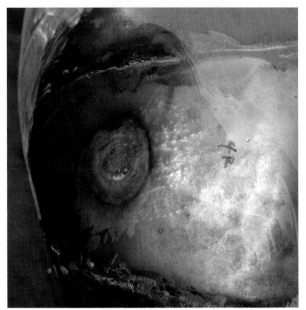

This is what the area should look like just after shrinking. Keep in mind that you can shrink more than one time near the same area if needed.

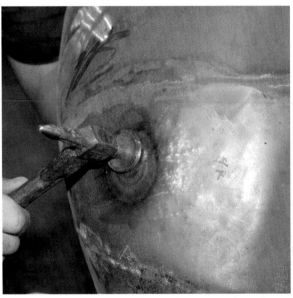

Simply tap the high spot a few times to drive the metal into the surrounding metal, making it thicker and "shrinking" the metal in that area. Do not hit it too hard. It does not take a lot of force to move the metal when it's hot.

surrounding area. By simply shrinking one section and having the surrounding area bend toward the shrink.

Now you're probably wondering *how* do you shrink metal? There are a number of ways to do this. One of the basics is to use a pick hammer with a padded dolly. Then there's the shrinking hammer and shrinking dolly, a shrinker, or an oxy-acetylene torch (hot-shrinking). In some ways a dent will shrink a surrounding panel by stretching it in a small area! Confused? Well imagine a rock hits the center of your door and puts a hemispherical dent in the metal. That rock has stretched the door metal at the area of impact, but the surrounding area has been pulled

toward the impact therefore shrinking the door skin in general. Now if you use a pick hammer (which is a small body hammer with one end pointed) and back the panel with a padded or rubber-coated dolly (or a block of wood), as you pick the panel you are basically shrinking the metal inward toward the work area but with greater control than using a rock.

The reason for using a block of wood instead of a steel dolly is that if you used metal for a backing then you will be stretching the metal, not shrinking it. Pounding metal between a hammer and a steel dolly tends to thin the metal and since metal has to go somewhere it expands outward into the surrounding metal. By using a soft block and a pick hammer, you allow the metal to form small peaks, thereby pulling the outer metal toward the small peaks.

I know that I might be oversimplifying this process, but doing so will make it easier to understand the process of shrinking, and the more you understand the better you can work metal. Just remember that for every action there is a reaction, so moving metal in one spot will cause the metal to move somewhere else. The trick is to know where the reaction will be and in what direction the metal will react. Then, and only then, will you have become the master over metal.

The process of shrinking metal with the use of a torch is well known and pretty standard—except for a new twist, which metal fabricator Ron Covell pointed out to me. He no longer recommends quenching, or accelerated cooling of the metal after shrinking it. The accepted method is (or was?) to find the area that needs to be shrunk, which would be a high spot in an otherwise smooth panel, then heat a small spot about the size of a silver dollar. Then, as it turns cherry red and raises to form a small bump, simply tap the bump down slightly until the spot is level with the surrounding metal. After which you would, but may not

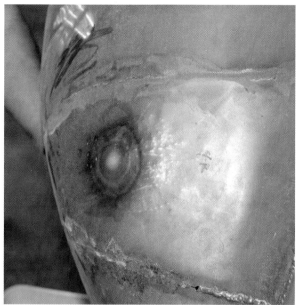

Cold shrinking is another method of bringing a piece of metal into a form you want. This is one of our pneumatic shrinkers that allows you to have both hands free as you work.

You will notice that as the metal heats it will expand and raise up in that area. Heat expands the metal, and this is just what you want. Hopefully, it will rise toward you or you will need to hit it from the bottom. On convex curves it will rise up, on concave surfaces it will move down.

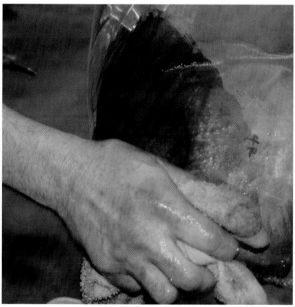

In the past we would always quench the metal with a wet rag, but in reality this tempers the metal in this area, making it unworkable unless it's annealed again. Metal should really be left to air cool.

A shrinking hammer and dolly work by roughing the surface and pulling the metal toward the tool. They do not pull a lot of metal and are only for light shrinks.

need to, dip a shop rag into a bucket of water and quench the spot. But what Ron told me, and I agree with him on this point, is that by quenching the spot, you will harden the metal at that spot. But if you do not use the quenching method and let the area cool off naturally, the metal can be worked later without having to anneal it again. On the other hand, Brian Hatano, the main fabricator in my shop, prefers to quench the metal and is able to attain the shape that he wants.

Stretching metal is the opposite of shrinking and produces the most common mistake that body men make when working, or overworking, a panel. It is the hammer-on-dolly work that thins and stretches the sheet of steel that requires shrinking it into its proper shape.

Remember, you can shrink metal a lot, it will only get thicker; but if you stretch it too much, it will then tear as it becomes too thin to have any tensile strength.

Whether shrinking or stretching a sheet of metal, you'll notice, if you're observant, that the worked area actually hardens. Why does the metal get hard after shrinking or stretching? We call this "work hardening" and it's the direct result of squeezing the molecules of metal so close together that the metal gets tougher and harder to work. If you run into this while working with metal, which I am sure you will, you can simply anneal the metal to soften it again.

In writing this book I came across the dilemma of explaining to the reader the problem of knowing when to shrink and when to stretch metal. Let's just say, for example, that you have an area in the front part of the hood that you just extended with a section of metal and, after welding it, wound up with metal that looks like the Pacific Ocean during a storm. You now have large sunken-in areas and you know you have to shrink or stretch them to pull them back to the original shape. Well which will it be: shrink or stretch?

So to solve this dilemma I can break it down to a simple example and a rule to help you remember: If the panel is flat and it has a large "oil can" in the center indicating too much metal, you would shrink the center area, pulling the excess area together into itself and as a result "tightening the metal" and removing the oil can effect. On the other hand, if the area has a large compound curve and the oil can is in the center of this curve you would stretch the metal, forcing it to stay in one direction as opposed to canning in and out.

So the simple rule would be: *for flat panels shrink; for curved panels stretch.*

Now, what if a section of metal has a very slight curve or is almost flat? Then I would start by slightly shrinking and if it gets worse then resort to stretching. Shrinking will thicken the metal, which can be stretched later, but stretching the metal will decrease the thickness and make it harder to work with if you need to shrink it later. If in doubt, shrink it first. Or, as I like to say, "error on the side of thicker."

Metal Stretching

Once again, for every action there is a reaction, and stretching metal in one spot will result in a buckling in another. To better understand the reaction concept I like to carry the example to the extreme with a whimsical example of a car that is hit in the front fender, now this car was absolutely perfect to start with in every dimension so that all the seams were 1/4-inch exactly. The average person would see a dent from the impact. But, the true scientist would notice that the small hit on the front fender closed the fender seam between the fender and the door a few thousandths of an inch and upon further measurement the rear door seam was slightly closed as well and no longer was exactly 0.2500000 inch, but 0.24999992 inch.

This is just for example and no car is that exact, but the point is that a simple tap in the front fender will result in every other part of the car being affected. So as you stretch metal in one area you should notice that the surrounding area is affected. In most cases this is just what you want so your action will cause the "desired effect" somewhere else. Once you understand the action/reaction concept you will have mastered working with metal.

Many times the area you need to work is not the area with the damage, but the result of the damaged area. Or it is near the damaged area and by working this area you will relieve the stress on the damaged area.

There are stretching tools on the market—I know because we manufacture a good metal stretcher—and they do a fine job around the edge of a panel, but sometimes you will need to stretch the center of a panel and the end stretchers just don't reach in far enough, so different methods are required. Among the ways to stretch metal, the most basic method is the "hammer-on-dolly" technique. This method requires that you place the dolly directly under the point where the hammer will strike so that each hit of the hammer compresses, or stretches, the metal.

How to Harden and Soften Metal

The simple process of hammering metal will compress the molecules and harden the metal. Then the simple process of heating the metal with a torch and letting it cool slowly will again allow the molecules to separate into their "own space" and once again be workable or soft. Now this is an oversimplification of the process of hardening and softening but it is the simplest way to describe a complex process. There is another way to harden metal and that is to heat it up and bring it down in temperature vary fast by dunking it in oil or water. So, with the simple differential of temperature range over a variable time frame you can control the hardness of a sheet of metal, making it workable or not.

The advantage of metal changing temperature is that the color of the metal changes with the temperature. With a sharp eye, you can control the temperature with a torch by moving it in and out and around. In most cases, you will be softening more than you harden the metal as the act of working metal will harden it for you and you will need to keep softening the area on a radically customized area. So learn how to soften well; this practice will be your best friend when the going gets tough (no pun intended).

The process of softening, or *annealing*, metal is a fairly simple one that involves heating and then cooling. Metal becomes annealed by heating it to its critical temperature — bright cherry red, or about 1200 degrees Fahrenheit—and then allowing it to slowly cool. The process of tempering metal, to make it harder and tougher, requires heating it up to its critical point and quenching it in water or oil.

To anneal sheet steel, you will have to heat it to a cherry red by constantly brushing the torch over the area until the metal is soft, then allowing it to cool slowly. This will take a bit of time and you should experiment on some old body metal to get the hang of it before working on your own car. It's easy for a novice to overheat and destroy a fender or other part of a car by over heating it and warping it. Only heat the area that you need to work and keep it to a minimum. Work slowly and keep the torch moving around. Also, use a rosebud tip that will give you a wide

The Oil Can Effect

If you've ever tried to make a part for your car out of a sheet of metal, or even used a small piece of metal for a patch panel as the metal comes from the metal yard, you may have noticed that after you start to weld it into place, the newly repaired section developed a tendency to flex excessively as you pushed on it. This is called the "oil can" effect. When you push even slightly on an oil-canned panel, it pops in with a metallic bang. Unless you're into sound effects and trying to create thunder, this is not a desirable attribute for any part of your car's body.

The oil can effect occurs at the moment that you begin to weld a patch into place. As soon as heat from the torch is applied, you'll start to see the metal taking the shape of Route 66 and the warping continues faster than you can control it. This is because it has no strength in and of itself, as a flat sheet.

A good welding technique minimizes the amount of oil-canning, but if you find yourself already in trouble, the metal will need to be reshaped a bit with a hammer and dolly, an English wheel to give it a slight crown for strength. If the piece is small enough and only being used to patch a rust area, then a sheet metal shrinker/stretcher can be used.

The shrinker/stretcher will allow you to take a flat piece of metal and, by bending it over something like the edge of a work table, or with a metal brake, form a 90-degree angle and then shrink or stretch one edge of the bent piece of metal to make it into a "dog leg" like the shape of the area around your windshield or the corner of your rear deck or doors.

After using the shrinker/stretcher on a piece of metal, you will notice that the metal has taken on more strength with this new form. If you need to make the outer trunk corner, you can just stretch the metal on its leg instead of shrinking it.

---

flame covering a broad area so as not to burn though in one spot.

It is a good idea to anneal aluminum prior to working it, as it will allow you to form the metal with ease. As you form the metal, you will find it getting harder and more difficult to shape. This is referred to as "work hardening" and is a result of the molecules in the metal being compressed together by repeated hammering or rolling in the English wheel. In either process, as the metal molecules are compressed together, the metal actually becomes more dense. Annealing the metal will allow the molecules to expand, thereby softening the metal.

Annealing aluminum, however, requires a slightly different approach, plus you will need to acquire some additional tools, such as a torch holder that can hold the oxy-acetylene torch head while you are moving the pieces of metal around. This is not an absolute necessity since you can simply turn the torch off and set it aside while you work the metal. The next tool is an annealing plate. This can be as simple as placing the metal on a homemade grate over an empty metal trash can.

The first step of the annealing process is to place the metal that needs to be annealed on the grate. Then I adjust the torch to an "acetylene-rich" setting by turning down the oxygen and lightly brush over the aluminum with

the flame. This will deposit black soot over the pieces of aluminum. This coating of soot serves as a temperature gauge as you heat the aluminum because it takes about 700 degrees from a neutral flame to burn off the soot. This is the ideal temperature required to anneal the aluminum. If more heat than that is applied, you will melt the aluminum.

Adjust the torch to a neutral flame and burn off the soot, moving the torch so you do not apply too much heat in one area, melting the metal. Slow circular paths will control the heat and burn off the soot. When you are done with the heating, the material can be quenched in water. This will be determined by the alloy, so check with the metal supply company on the particular metal you are using to find the proper method of annealing. The area should now be annealed. A simple bend of the edge of the sheet will prove this.

Tools For Metal Shaping and Fabrication

Basically, there are only two places where you can fabricate with a large sheet of metal and have adequate working space: on the floor or on a table. I recommend the latter for obvious reasons. A perfectly flat layout table measuring 4 feet wide by at least 8 feet long (preferably 10 feet, since full sheets of metal are 10 feet long) with

This is a mandrel tubing bender. This machine will only give you a predetermined radius, depending on the dies you use. It is very handy for roll cages.

A universal holding stand is also a useful tool for either painting parts or working on parts. This is an Eastwood product.

Pedestal grinders are also scattered around the shop and are must-have tools for sharpening and grinding of metal.

Some tools come in cans, such as the rattle can paint prep, guide coat and primer. Spray cans are not that bad if you need a quick shot of primer or guide coat and do not have the time to mix a batch and put it in your gun.

good illumination is one of the main fabricator's "tools." You'll do 99 percent of your measuring, cutting, forming, trimming and mock up on this table so it's best to get, or build, a good sturdy one. If you choose to build a layout table, you'll soon discover that full sheets of metal come in 10-foot lengths, while sheets of wood for a table top are only 8 feet long. You can solve this dilemma like my dad did in his shop: by making fold-down leafs at each end of the table. The leafs can be folded up or down depending on the surface size that your metal requires.

A second level, or shelf, can be added about midway between the floor and the top of the table. This area can serve as storage for your unused sheets, tools and patterns, as they will be out of the way, yet conveniently within reach when you need them. You may also want to attach electrical and regulated air outlets to the table so you can quickly plug in for power. A good table will also have heavy-duty casters—two locking swivel casters at one end, and two non-swivel casters at the opposite end.

It has been said that the only difference between man

We have an assortment of cutoff or chop saws at the shop. Instead of changing blades for steel, aluminum or wood, we have a different saw for each material.

This is a Porter Cable metal cutting saw that will cut through a 6-inch steel bar with ease.

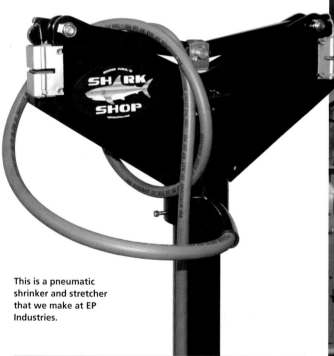

This is a pneumatic shrinker and stretcher that we make at EP Industries.

The Care and Feeding of Tools

All of this talk about tools brings up another point (actually, a major pet peeve of mine) which, hopefully, some of my employees will read. Once you are finished with a tool, especially if it's a borrowed tool, clean it up and replace the blade or drill or whatever part is now worn out so it will be ready to use the next time you need it. I get so frustrated when I go to get a socket and the one I need is the only one missing, or one of the drill bits is missing out of the index because someone was too lazy to put them away. Then I'm left to either find another one, or run to the store to buy a new one.

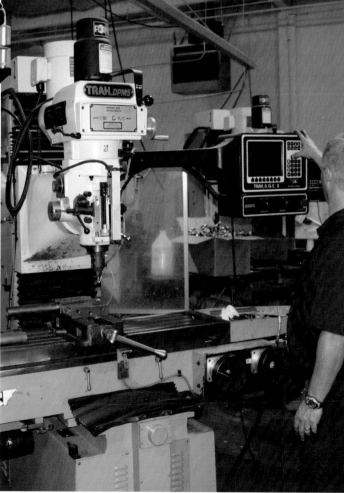

If you are a member of the more money than brains club and have enough work to support it, a good CNC mill is very handy for not only prototyping, but small production runs of that custom bracket or part that you made and everyone wants.

Bend Pak lifts are found throughout our shop and are seldom empty. This is a two-post lift.

This in one of our "P-dollies" that is mounted in a vice on wheels. P-dollies come in most radiuses and are very handy for shaping metal or small tubing as one end has grooves for bending tubes to what ever radius you need.

Masking machines save the newspaper for the dog and will save you the hassle of taping along the edge of the paper.

Hammers are like clamps; you can't have too many. Start off with a basic ball or cross peen hammer with a weight of 2 or 3 lbs., and then add your specialty hammers such as a deadblow, leather mallet, etc. Most hammers for fabricating have dual-purpose heads.

Eastwood makes a manual shrinker/stretcher that is very affordable for the beginner and can mount on any flat surface. We mount them together because we use them together.

and animal is that we use tools and they don't. While not entirely true—some animals have been known to use tools—I will offer an alternative euphemism: The difference between man and animal is that while animals use tools to live, men live to use tools.

Building your set of tools can turn into an addiction of sorts, but it begins out of necessity. It's frustrating to be right in the middle of a project and not have that one extra "C" clamp. Clamps are like additional hands to a fabricator and I've found that you can't have too many. There is no set number of clamps that I can recommend for you to get. Suffice it to say that I have more than a hundred clamps of

If you're on a shoestring budget and can only afford one set at a time, always opt for the metric wrench and socket set first, since metric sizes will fit all SAE sizes, but not vice-versa. This goes for both wrenches and sockets. I prefer 12-point wrenches, while my sockets are 6-point.

Quarter-inch and 3/8-inch drive ratchet and socket sets in metric and SAE sizes.

This is a plastic teardrop mallet and a sandbag. Start with a medium-sized mallet and add the smaller and larger sizes as you progress. A leather sandbag used to form metal on can be filled with sand or lead shot. I use sand in my shop.

An assortments of sanding blocks will help you straighten the body of almost any car.

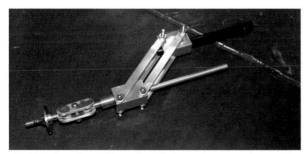

This is our newest tool for marking holes on uneven surfaces, such as fenders. It allows you to mark a perfect hole on a slanted surface.

Dual-action (DA) sanders are sold in almost every price range, so you can buy a cheap one that will last a few years, or a more expensive one that you can hand down to your kids someday. I am still using some of my dad's tools.

If you're working with metal, you will have to grind and sand frequently. Assuming that you have an air compressor, a pneumatic 5-inch sander/grinder is the most versatile. You can use fiber discs or carbide wheels with it and they're fairly inexpensive.

Locking pliers are commonly called Vise Grips. The C-clamp style Vise Grip is available in several sizes and is standard equipment for automotive customizing.

If you don't have air yet, you can use a 4 1/2-inch electric angle grinder. These are a bit more cumbersome, but they get the job done.

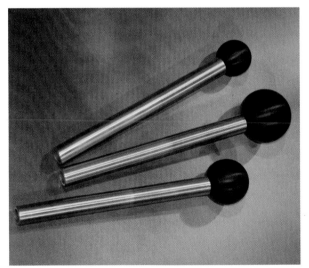

Ball hammers are used for shaping metal, much like the teardrop hammer except you do not have to keep these in the proper rotation. You just grab one and pound.

various sizes and configurations and sometimes I still need another clamp or two. But when it comes to the use of tools, I have a couple of rules that I try to abide by.

Rule number one concerning tools: "**Don't borrow tools—buy them**"! If you make a living using tools, don't let this become an issue where you work. People that borrow tools are annoying to tool owners for several reasons. Borrowers do not respect tools because they did not fork out the hard-earned cash to buy them for themselves and they very rarely replace tools when they are worn out or broken. They will just quickly put them back in your toolbox, and lay other tools on top of them so you will not

notice that the tool they used was broken.

Occasionally, I make an exception to this rule by hiring a worker who has a lot of potential but very few tools. This always comes back to haunt me when I discover broken or missing tools in my box. Maybe rule number one should be, "Don't loan tools!"

Rule number two concerning tools: **The quality and quantity of tools that one has reflects the quality and quantity of work one is capable of doing.** I have noticed that the people who come to work for me either buy tools or do not, and that the ones that don't, or make a minimum purchase of cheap tools, generally do not last.

We also make a larger English wheel/planishing hammer for the serious body man.

We use transmission jacks for things like holding up front valances during construction (when the car is on a lift) or holding the side rockers up for welding. You need to use tools for more than the intended purpose to be a good customizer.

Different wheel anvils are available for the Eddie Paul English wheel with a low to high crown.

The ones that buy tools are making an investment in their own future and by purchasing tools, are showing that they have a genuine interest in customizing and are planning on staying around, at least until the tools are paid off. Over the past 35 years in the customizing business, I've accumulated quite an assortment of tools, but I still find new tools to buy on a regular basis.

A lot of tools generally indicate a person that knows how to do a lot of things; few tools or no tools indicates a person that generally does not know how to use tools and is just passing through. Would you show up at a gunfight without a gun? Well don't show up for work without tools!

With the recent onslaught of do-it-yourself shows, everybody seems to be getting their hands dirty once again fixing up their cars, homes and yards. And thanks to shows such as Discovery Channel's "Monster Garage" and "American Chopper," America now has a renewed fascination with customized machines. Both men and

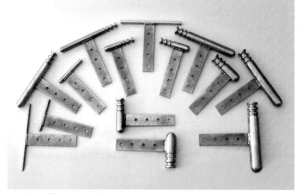

We also offer a set of what we call "P-dollies" that are radiused on one end and flat on the other end. They have a set of grooves machined in the flat end that are perfect for bending tubing or taking a dent out of a bead.

women are now working on their own motorcycles and cars, and I will do my best to support them with the knowledge of what kind of tools they need and how to use them.

The current "hot" television programs show you how to build a monster lawn mower from a car, or fabricate a custom motorcycle from an old beer can, but they do not cover the tools the auto shops use for their creations. The viewer's interest has been sparked; it's now time to take the

A rolling table is another handy item in the shop as you can roll it to the job if needed. We made this one in about a day and it has a 1/4-inch sheet of steel for a top.

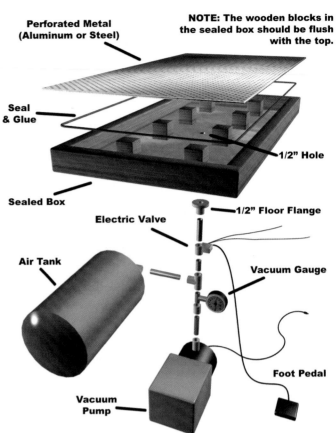

Perforated Metal (Aluminum or Steel)

NOTE: The wooden blocks in the sealed box should be flush with the top.

Seal & Glue

1/2" Hole

Sealed Box

1/2" Floor Flange

Electric Valve

Air Tank

Vacuum Gauge

Foot Pedal

Vacuum Pump

This illustration shows the schematic for a basic vacuum forming machine that can be built at home for a few hundred dollars.

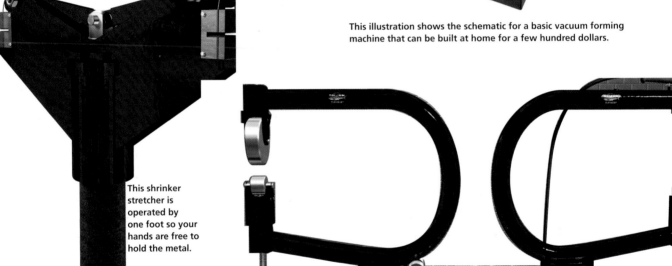

This shrinker stretcher is operated by one foot so your hands are free to hold the metal.

A FLAT
B - 5 5/8 RADIUS
B1 - 3 3/8 RADIUS
C - 2 1/4 RADIUS
C1 - 1 5/8 RADIUS
D - 1 1/4 RADIUS

A radius gauge helps determine the curve of a shaped piece of metal.

This is a planishing hammer/English wheel that we make for the Eastwood Company and sell direct to the public. It will handle most small to medium-size jobs for most garage and shop work.

A Beverly shear is just a giant set of tin snips with a lot of leverage and a way of mounting the unit to the floor. This will allow you to cut heavy gauge metal with ease.

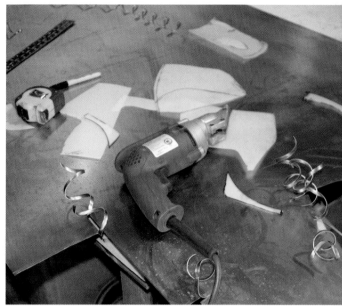
Electric shears are one of the handiest tools for rough cutting of sheet metal up to 16 gauge. Keep in mind they remove about an 1/8-inch strip of metal as they cut.

Sharp, heavy-duty scissors and cutters are required for cutting patterns.

Small lead-filled bags are useful for holding, propping and support while you're beating on a sheet of metal.

wheel and really show them what tools to own and how to use them in their own garage. In this chapter I plan to do just that or at least move you into the right direction so you can make an informed decision next time you stroll through a tool store and not just buy a tool because it looks cool in your toolbox drawer.

It is amazing that some people don't know how to use even the simplest of tools even though they may own them. Do you know how to use a pickle fork to remove your ball joints? Or smooth out a rough spot in a splash apron using a planishing hammer, or even an English wheel? By the way, how is your knowledge of the Super Pro Plus stud welder? Do you have enough draw pins to complete the

job? Or do you own your own finger brake? It is equally amazing that some tool manufacturers do not include a basic set of instructions for their tools. It almost makes you wonder if they know how to use the tools themselves.

Hopefully this book will help show how the proper tool is used and what makes the difference between an amateur job and a professional job.

Years ago, as a teen, I purchased an arc welder and paid it off on my first welding job. By the second job I owned the welder and the money I made on the job became pure profit. This basic logic has filled my shop with tools…and tools make money! But only if you know how to use them.

A set of body hammers and dollies are a must for fabricators. The are numerous dolly shapes and hammer configurations, each of which are designed for specific contours, working positions, smoothing, shrinking, dinging, etc. Tool companies such as Snap-On, The Eastwood Company, and Craftsman usually sell the most useful hammers and dollies in kit form.

Side cutters of the high-leverage type will serve many uses.

A 25- to 30-foot tape measure and a few straight-edge and square measuring sets are nice to have on hand.

A box of Sharpie fine-point felt tip markers.

An accurate torpedo level with a magnetic base.

A medium-sized pry bar will take the place of that screwdriver you've been using.

The Top 20 Tools For Fabricating

1 A 25- to 30-foot tape measure and a few straight-edge and square measuring sets.

2 An accurate torpedo level with a magnetic base.

3 A pair of sharp, heavy-duty scissors for cutting patterns.

4 A box of Sharpie fine-point felt tip markers.

5 Hammers. Hammers are like clamps; you can't have too many. Start off with a basic ball or cross peen hammer with a weight of 2 or 3 lbs., and then add your specialty hammers such as a deadblow, leather mallet, etc. Insist on good quality here with heads that are securely attached to the handle. Most hammers for fabricating have dual-purpose heads (i.e. a pick hammer has a flat, round head on one side with a long narrow pick at the other). If a hammer has a claw on one end, it's for pounding nails, not for fabricating.

6 Plastic teardrop mallet and a sandbag. Start with a medium-sized mallet and add the smaller and larger sizes as you progress. A leather sandbag used to form metal on can be filled with sand or lead shot. I use sand in my shop.

7 A set of slip-joint pliers such as Channellocks are invaluable.

8 Side cutters of the high-leverage type will serve many uses.

9 A medium-sized pry bar to take the place of that screwdriver you've been using.

10 A set of body hammers and dollies are a must for fabricators. The are numerous dolly shapes and hammer configurations, each of which are designed for specific contours, working positions, smoothing, shrinking, dinging, etc. Tool companies such as Snap-On, The Eastwood Company, and Craftsman usually sell the most useful hammers and dollies in kit form.

11 Clamps and locking pliers. Of course, locking pliers are what we refer to as Vise Grips. The C-clamp style Vise Grip is available in several sizes and is standard equipment for automotive customizing.

12 Pneumatic 5-inch sander/grinder. If you're working with metal, you will have to grind and sand frequently. Assuming that you have an air compressor, this type of grinder is the most versatile. You can use fiber discs or carbide wheels with it and they're fairly inexpensive. My fabricator here in the shop has six of these tools ready to use at all times, each fitted with different abrasives.

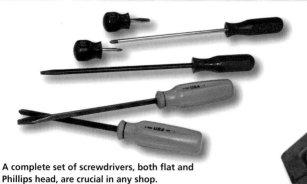

A complete set of screwdrivers, both flat and Phillips head, are crucial in any shop.

A basic hack saw with spare blades is all you really need to start with, but it won't be long before you'll want to use power.

Hand shears and tin snips are must-have tools. Most fabricators start off making all of their cuts with these hand tools. They will still be useful even after you graduate to power shears.

A set of slip-joint pliers such as Channellocks are invaluable.

A sand bag, or shot bag, and teardrop or ball hammer are used for rough shaping of metal.

13 If you don't have air yet, you can use a 4 1/2-inch electric angle grinder. These are a bit more cumbersome, but they get the job done. Cheaper models tend to slow down too much under load. Look for an amperage rating of no less than 5. Like the pneumatic 5-inch grinder, this is a great all-purpose tool for grinding and shaping metal, dealing with rusty hardware and more.

14 Electric metal shears. In my humble opinion, electric metal shears are far superior to their pneumatic counterparts. They're also more expensive. The Bosch 1500C is a two-bladed shear rated for up to 16-gauge mild steel, has a tight turning radius and makes clean cuts. Three-bladed shears are good for straight or large-radius cuts, however, the three-blade-type removes a thin strip of material as it cuts.

15 Hand shears and tin snips. Most fabricators start off making all of their cuts with these hand tools. They will still be useful even after you graduate to power shears. Tin snips with the yellow grips are used for straight cuts, green grips for left cuts, and red grips for right. Upright aviation snips have similarly color-coded grips, but they cut with a unique push/pull cutting action and can turn or rotate while cutting circles. Uprights provide easier and safer cutting in tight spaces and overhead.

16 Combination wrench sets in metric and SAE sizes. If you're on a shoestring budget and can only afford one set at a time, always opt for the metric set first since metric sizes will fit all SAE sizes, but not vice-versa. This goes for both wrenches and sockets. I prefer 12-point wrenches while my sockets are 6-point.

17 1/4-inch-drive and 3/8-inch-drive ratchet and socket set in metric and SAE sizes.

18 A complete set of screwdrivers, both flat and Phillips head. Most likely, many of the flat-tipped drivers will serve double duty as a prying tool once in awhile. We all do this with our screwdrivers, but for the record, always use the proper tool for the job.

19 Saws. A basic hacksaw with spare blades is all you really need to start with, but it won't be long before you'll want to use power.

20 Vixen files. Power grinders can take the place of standard hand files when it comes to deburring or edge-trimming, but there is one type of file that a grinder can't replace. That's the vixen file. The vixen file is a special tool that is an absolute necessity for metal finishing.

If I don't end this list of basic starter tools right here, I'll more than likely end up putting every tool that I own on it because I feel that every tool that I own is a necessity. There are probably a few more that should be included, such as a couple of die grinders with carbide rotary bits, an air nibbler and a saber saw, but you can add these tools later.

Metal is easy to cut with the right tool. Metal cutting/

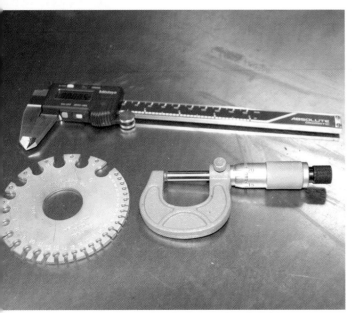

On the top is a set of digital calipers and on the left is a gauge wheel. This shows three ways to check the gauge of metal, so you have no excuse to not get it right.

This wheel has slits that you simply match to the metal.

shearing tools include hand sheers, stomp snips, air hammer with panel-cutting bit, abrasive cut-off wheels, oxy-acetylene torches, plasma cutters, nibblers, and pneumatic as well as electric saws. The bottom line is that there just isn't "one tool" that can handle all of your cutting needs. In fact, you will often use two different tools on a single cut just to make a right or left turn. But basically, cutters are designed to shear, nibble, melt or grind away metal.

Burning your way through metal with a torch is as much fun as it is easy and it's very likely the best way for roughing a large piece of metal into a more manageable size. For years, fabricators relied on the oxygen-acetylene cutting torch, not the most precise method, but it's portable, requires no power, and is relatively inexpensive. The hot ticket for tool cutting now is the plasma cutter. Plasma cutters use an electric arc with compressed air to cut metal. Neat, clean and very intricate cuts are possible with just a little bit of practice.

The plasma arc is a cold burn (that is, it does not require heating the metal until it's red hot), but I would not recommend touching the metal directly after the cut. As a result of its cold burn, sheet metal will be relatively warp-free and cool to the touch within a few minutes. Another benefit of the plasma cutter is that you can actually cut a painted panel without damaging the paint. Plasma cutting metal thicknesses over a 1/4 inch should be done with a larger 220-volt machine, but 110-volt units can easily handle sheet metal.

Abrasive cutoff wheels in 3-, 4-, and 5-inch diameters are versatile tools when used in conjunction with a die grinder motor (either straight or right-angle type). Five-inch wheels should be used on a larger grinder motor and all of these tools should be equipped with a deflector shield. Abrasive cut-off wheels are merely thin versions of a standard high-speed metal grinding wheel. A high-speed cut-off or grinding wheel will have a reinforced abrasive composition to minimize the chance of shattering during use.

Measure Twice, Cut Once!

While fabricating any part, periodic checking for fit of the surrounding parts is key to good customizing. Just think of the term "custom fit." You will find that as you add a piece of metal to your car's body, it may begin to overlap in some spots and fall a little short in others. This is especially true when working with larger pieces with compound curves. As you weld a piece of metal into your car, it is not that uncommon to have it pull into a weld, bend, stretch or just move around a little, so be prepared to do constant trimming or adjusting as you weld. Look ahead to see if it is starting to move around and trim it early if you can so the snips will still grab the metal. If you wait too long you will not be able to get the tip of your snips in to the edge of the metal and you will have to resort to other means of trimming such as a plasma cutter. You may also try tack welding the piece around the perimeter so it will stay in alignment as you weld it permanently in place.

After a while you will know which way metal will move and about how far it will move. It is at this point that you are starting to master the art of metal forming and on you way to becoming a metal fabricator. We constantly try to predict which way metal will go in particular situations and we are not always right, but even through our miss-guesses we learn to predict the direction and amount it will move the next time we apply heat or a hammer and dolly. Metal work is a constant amalgamation of education, experimentation and experience. It is not a skill you are born with or can pick up by reading a single book. It is a skill that will take years to master and more years to perfect.

Tools For Welding and Cutting

Welding is the process of heating metal up to a point that allows the melting and fusion of molecules between two separate sheets into one. There are a number of ways to achieve the required heat. One way is by igniting a combination of flammable gases; another is through the use of electricity to create an arc by grounding out the rod (or wire), or by creating a plasma to induce a heat source, then adding a filler rod of a similar material to the open gap. This is probably a little more than you care to know at this point.

Selecting a welder requires some careful thought. Some things that you'll have to take into consideration are: your budget, the application and power availability. There are several manufacturers that offer a complete line of welders, but rather than reviewing every machine available, we'll take a look at some of the welders that I use in my shop. Since we handle everything from heavy production welding to light sheet-metal patch jobs with all types of metal, the welding equipment that I use covers just about every application that you will likely encounter. The final choice all depends on your particular needs, application and source of power.

There are several types of welders that a professional fabricator is capable of using. There's basic gas welding with an oxygen-acetylene torch, there's the arc welder (also called a "stick welder" or "buzz box"), there's Heliarc (also called TIG, or tungsten-inert-gas welding), and last but not least, MIG (metal-inert-gas) welding. For all intents and purposes, MIG welding is the fabricator's number one choice for many reasons, and this is the form of welding that I'll focus on.

But first, I'm going to take a little different approach in helping you select a welder by starting with your power source. Everyone that has electricity has 110AC. Some of us might even have 220AC, but the question is, do you have access to that 220 or is it tucked away behind your washing machine? Running an extension cord with number-2 cables could set you back quite a bit and then you are limited to the distance and type of plug you can use. If you take the welder to another shop or garage it more than likely will not be the same plug you have on your welder. So if you are working on a normal car made of sheet metal and not a Sherman tank made from 2-inch-thick, hardened steel,

We have a huge assortment of welders and plasma cutters in our shop. With the amount of welding we do, we need them all.

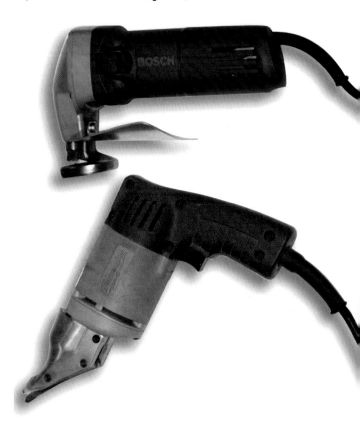

In my opinion, electric metal shears are far superior to their pneumatic counterparts. They're also more expensive. The Bosch 1500C is a two-bladed shear rated for up to 16-gauge mild steel, has a tight turning radius, and makes clean cuts. Three-bladed shears are good for straight or large-radius cuts; however, the three-blade-type removes a thin strip of material as it cuts.

Chapter Two

Body Repair Basics For Customizing— Getting Off to a Smooth Start

This could be a great first car for a project if it has rust. Rust will bring the price way down and keep you from destroying a restorable classic.

This rusted-out 1972 Mustang fastback was only $600. You can see how rust reduced not only the structural integrity, but the price as well.

Pick the Right Car For Your Project

This is the easy part of customizing because there are no guidelines. You can pick whatever car you like. It's the condition of the car that you must scrutinize over, because it will serve as the foundation for every modification that you have in store. When I was young only a two-door was an acceptable body style for customizing and of the many two-door models available, only certain years, makes and models were on the "in list." Today the list is wide open and in many cases finding some obscure oddball turns out to be the best subject for a custom. Studebakers, Impala station wagons, Ford Galaxies, and the hoards of imports are now deemed acceptable for customizing.

That being said, I would still start with one of the more popular models, but possibly go with an off year that has a lower value. For example, you could pick up a '72 or '73 Chevelle for substantially less money than a prime 1970 model would cost and the body lines are virtually identical. The areas where a noticeable difference exists—the headlights and taillights—would most likely be the things you would change anyway. Also, when purchasing a car with the sole intent of customizing the body, you can save money by avoiding performance models.

I found a 1940 Ford Deluxe four-door sedan for about $3,000 on the Internet. It was located back east so the body had "a bit" of rust and was a perfect car for this book. If I

This is a 1972 Mustang fastback and a great car to start with—as are almost any Mustang fastbacks. This will soon be a very radical custom car. I picked this car up for about $6,000.

were looking for a restoration project, I would have passed on this car as it was not "all there"; a few parts were missing and large sections of the floorboard had rusted away, no doubt scattered along some desolate highway some time ago. The decrepit condition of this old Ford would certainly be a major disappointment to anybody else who

This is an example of a fast custom: two weeks for six cars, including the engines and brakes, as well as the paint. Each car was used as a stunt car.

This is the interior of one of the *xXx* cars. Some of the stunt cars had Coke cans on the dash for gauges—crude, but at 100 mph, who could tell?

bought it, but for me and my crew—who tagged it as not a rust bucket, but a rust barrel!—it would be the recipient of many custom modifications and repairs.

So that's the brief history of the not-so-hot rod that you'll be seeing throughout this book. When we're finished with it, it'll be nothing less than a full-on custom 1940 Ford like no other in the world! I'm positive that the seller must have thought I was nuts to buy this heap sight unseen. I think I sounded almost excited to find that the rust had gotten the

best of the car, and that all the parts were not there, or that the grille was replaced with a screen. None of this mattered, as it was going to be customized and the main thing was that the price was within my budget, and it was exactly what I was looking for.

Most '40s era vehicles had lots of big, rounded body panels and the best part of an old car like this is that it's made of heavy metal (18 gauge). With solid metal like this (except, of course, for the floor and a few spots along the doors), it was wide open for cosmetic surgery and I was the doctor. Another thing that I like about building up an old car is that it's exempt from the strict California emissions regulations that late-model cars must adhere to. This would be the perfect car to receive one of the supercharged Chevy engines sitting out in the shop!

With a blown power plant in mind, the tone of the '40 Ford build-up would definitely have to be one of performance, yet I wanted to incorporate some traditional customizing along with some new ideas. My first thought was that I would chop, channel and section it to the ground to make it one of the lowest cars ever built, but then my practical side kicked in and I stepped back a little. I want this to be a showstopper but not a "trailer queen;" it must be comfortable and practical to drive on a daily basis. So I decided that I would still do a radical chop on the top, but the channeling and sectioning would have to be more on the subtle side. I could drop the floorboard (what little is left of it!) to gain extra legroom and then box the frame

Eddie Paul's Custom Bodywork Handbook

This is the way my '40 Ford looked the day it came into the shop. It was even rougher than I expected.

As I looked closer I could tell why the previous owner sold it. Under that layer of dust was a bit of surface rust but most was hidden by the trim.

The bumpers were straight, but the chrome had long since disappeared. The grille was made out of screen, but none of this mattered because this was to be a full-on custom anyway and all this would be replaced with new metal.

for extra strength. I also planned to clip the front portion of the frame in favor of a later model. The '40's straight front axle with its "buggy spring" suspension might have provided a plush ride 65 years ago, but like I said, this was not a resto.

But I still wanted to do something different, hopefully something no one had ever tried before. As the wheels turned in my head, I made notes of ideas along with rough sketches of things I could try. Then it occurred to me, the psychology behind building custom cars is not unlike the state of mind behind building movie cars. The cars that

my shop built for *xXx* and *The Fast and the Furious* came together as a result of a mad thrash to meet a crazy deadline. I know that some shops take weeks, if not months, to do a custom car. We did 80, yes, that's eight-zero, within a time span of one month. Granted we worked long days, nights and weekends, but when you calculate 80 cars in a month to cars per day, that's record book material! And if you saw the movies, it's plain to see that the cars looked pretty good.

On the other hand, I've had several non-movie cars in the shop for what seemed like an eternity, tending to every

Aside from a very light scrape, the fenders were in reasonable shape and the car still had the original hubcaps.

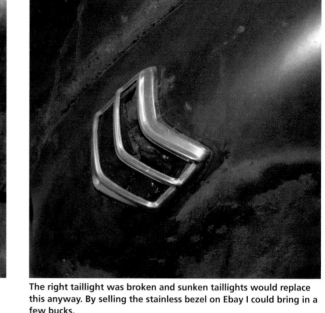

The right taillight was broken and sunken taillights would replace this anyway. By selling the stainless bezel on Ebay I could bring in a few bucks.

The drip rail that runs above the windows was all but gone and the seam between the roof and the body was pretty rusty as well, but not beyond repair.

The interior was all original but not in the best of shape. If this were to be a restoration I would be feeling pretty sick about now. Since it was going to be full-on custom, all I needed was about 3 square feet of original metal to start with and I could build the rest.

little detail, polishing the paint to a high luster, and when it was finished, I'd be hard-pressed to tell the difference in paint jobs between it and one of the *Fast and Furious* tuner cars. An exaggeration? Well, maybe, but I still wonder why some of the "quick and dirty" movie cars that we build come out so good when our attention to detail and quality isn't nearly that which we put into a real customer's car. The psychology of customizing, if there is such a thing, is this: the less encumbered you are by fear of close examination, the smoother the job goes. It's not that we don't care about details and quality when we build cars for the movies, we know that if it looks good from 20 feet away, it'll look awesome on the big screen. So we approach cars for movies

on a whole different level; one of getting it done on or before the deadline. Knowing that a paint job doesn't have to be absolutely perfect results in a paint job that comes out quite well because of the relaxed approach. This is why I prefer to start my personal customizing projects with a cheap car that would otherwise be a tire-spin away from the car crusher, which is exactly what my '40 Ford is.

There are many different approaches to customizing a car. At one end of the spectrum is the guy who must know exactly what the finished car will look like down to the smallest detail. A professional illustration is part of the pre-build and no part of the job deviates from the planned attack. On the other end is the spontaneous method by the

The seats were removed with a pry bar as the bolts were too rusty to even find. It was at this point that I started to get a bit concerned.

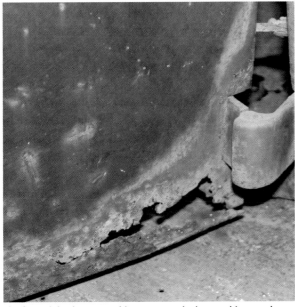

The front right door was a bit rusty near the bottom hinge and would have to be restored, but this was child's play compared to the rest of the project.

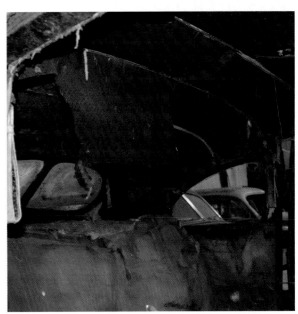

This is the view that was not shown in the ad when I bought the car, but really would not have mattered, anyway. All this rusty metal was destined to hit the dumpster.

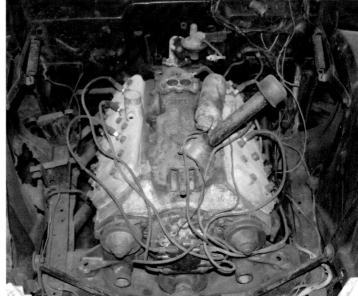

The old Flathead engine definitely needed some work.

When wrenches don't work you will need to resort to power, and an abrasive cut-off tool can "unbolt" many of the parts on a car.

The first step in replacing the floor was to clear out all the loose metal and assess how much damage the water did to the floor and the frame.

guy who can jump right in and go for it. Although I can't just "go for it" with a customer's car, I do with my own. Some of my wildest ideas have come about this way and no amount of planning and sticking to a plan could've made it better. I once cut up and customized a vintage, low-mileage 1966 Mustang 2+2 (that's a fastback for you non-pony car people). I grafted the widest rear flares that I could fill with tires on the rear fenders and continued to modify the car from every conceivable angle. It was worthless as a classic, but it made it into all the car magazines and onto a couple of television shows as well. And when I sold it several years later, I got more for it than I would have if I simply restored it. My point here is that selecting the right car and

customizing it tastefully using the proper techniques will only increase its value.

Once you know what year, make and model car that you want, you still have to make a choice out of the ones that are available. The best approach for this is to have a general idea of what your customizing entails so that you can avoid spending more than you have to. For example, if you know that you are going to put a different engine in the car, then it makes no sense to buy one with a built engine or even one with an engine at all. The same applies to interiors, the body, wheels and tires, etc. If you apply this approach successfully when buying your car, you'll end up with extra cash to spend on tools and materials for the project.

Bruce started by cutting off the bolts that hold the floorboard down. We tried to remove them, but they were too far gone.

Carpet tends to hold the moisture longer than metal, so it will keep the rust alive after you think the car is dry.

The plan was to weld the trunk up solid to the body so the trunk gutter could be cut out, removing the rust as well.

Body Repair Basics For Customizing—Getting Off to a Smooth Start

When I was shopping for that '40 Ford, a typical dialogue with a potential seller would go something like this: "Hello, I'm interested in buying your car. I don't really care about the tires, wheels, engine, trans, rear end, interior, dash, grille, or glass. Also if it has rust, just let me know the extent of it." I might explain that the car is going to be customized extensively, and if the seller is negotiable, he could keep the parts that I don't need to lower the price. It took me just a few calls before I had a car because I knew what I wanted and what I was going to do to it.

Challenges serve as a motivating element for me when I do a custom. I like the challenge of making a car look like something that it's not. It's easy to enhance the style of a car, but when you want to change it altogether into something entirely different or new, that's a challenge! I once transformed a customer's Volvo into a very real-looking "Rolls Royce." Another good one was an Austin Healy that I converted into an AC Cobra-style car with widened fenders and a 392 Hemi for power. On the milder side, we do a lot of subtle "cloning" of cars here in my shop, like making convertibles out of hardtops or a '67 GTO out of a '66 LeMans.

This is the car for the 1987 film *Inner Space*. It had to run as good as it looked, so we gave it a brand-new engine, as well as a new top and interior.

you sandblast, sand will get into every part of your car. You'll be vacuuming sand for as long as you own the car. Also, blasting can generate enough heat on a panel to warp the metal. Experienced sandblasting shops know how to blast car bodies to avoid this, but many do not. The ones that do will charge you accordingly. I have a sandblasting cabinet and portable blasters in my shop for spot blasting small parts, but I don't recommend it for major rust on car bodies.

Metal Treatments, Coatings and Preparation

Before I get too far off track, let's get back to customizing! Before I do any of the modifications to the '40 Ford that I bought, there's the issue of rust. There are minor rust spots on some of the panels, and major rust on others. There are a number of ways to deal with rust but, unfortunately, none that I know of can magically transform rust back into metal. A book on restoration will go into great detail on the subject of rust but quite frankly, talking about rust is about as enlightening as watching it so I'll cut it down to just the facts.

There are a variety of ways to deal with rust. It can be as simple as a vigorous scrubbing with a wire brush followed by some naval jelly. Sandblasting can effectively stop rust, too, but as with wire brushing, there are limitations. If

Minor Rust Repair

Rust that can be topically treated, either by chemical, spot blasting or wire brush method falls into the minor rust category. Chemicals that include naval jelly, metal etching solutions and special coatings formulated to encapsulate rust all work well providing you follow the instructions. If you choose the wire brush or an abrasive disc, I recommend that you follow up with a metal etching solution. Grinding may remove surface corrosion but, even though you're down to what looks like bare shiny metal, rust might still exist.

If the rust on your metal appears to be just a light oxidation that can be course-sanded or wire brushed, there is another potential problem to be aware of. The high-speed rotary tool that you must use can create excessive heat and warp the panel if you concentrate the work in one spot too long. To prevent this, move the tool around constantly as you sand or brush.

This '50 Merc was one of the four built for the movie *Cobra* in just 14 days; it was then wrecked in just a few minutes and restored in about two years. Of course, we did not work on it each day.

The front end of the "Awsom 50" was almost reconstructed from scratch due to rust and abuse from stunts.

Flashy bolt-on cosmetics are easy to install and inexpensive for film cars. On a true custom, we would fabricate pieces like this.

This is the last time I saw the *Cobra* car. It just hit a pipe ramp in one of the many stunts during the film.

Now this was a real find—the 1950 Merc used in the movie *Cobra*. I should know because I built the cars for the movie and also restored this one when it was brought into my shop years later.

On my rusty old '40 we found the whole floor needed replacing, so we stripped it down to the frame.

A 4 x 4-foot sheet of cardboard was laid down on the frame and marked along the frame rails for a pattern.

Some of the bolts could be removed by a set of Vise Grips and some Liquid Wrench, but most had to be cut off with a grinder.

This pattern was then trimmed along the lines and reinstalled in the car.

There are a number of rust removers, preventive chemicals and rust-removing tools on the market, but sometimes there is no hope and the metal has to be replaced.

Wire brushing can be accomplished with a hand brush or with a small wire wheel mounted on an electric or air drill. In terms of heat build-up and warpage, these are perhaps your safest bets, but they can be time consuming. Minor rust is fairly easy to remove, but will return if the problem that caused it is not thoroughly eliminated. So remember to fix the problem and not just remove surface rust.

The causes of rust are almost infinite, and can be as basic and unavoidable as a poor design on the part of the auto manufacturer. A lot of '60s and '70s era GM cars were highly prone to rust around the rear window where water tended to collect under the window trim. It wasn't until the late '70s that factory undercoating became a standard practice. Rust can be the result of a harsh environment such as salted roads during the snow season. And saltwater areas are common

The pattern does not need to be the entire length of the floor. You can add sections as you go to increase the length. This will make it easier to work with the small pieces, rather than one large sheet.

Again, I marked the transmission cutout on the cardboard, following the front frame rail back.

I then moved to the other side and filled in that section of the floor with a pattern made from cardboard.

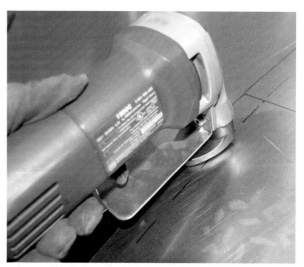

Using an electric shear, the metal was cut on the lines and ready to roll. Flanges were marked at about 1 inch from each side, so I had a way to weld it to the floor.

As seen from the front, the rear section was cut to allow for the driveshaft well to be welded in.

A simple 3-foot slip roll was used to roll the driveshaft well plates into the radius I needed.

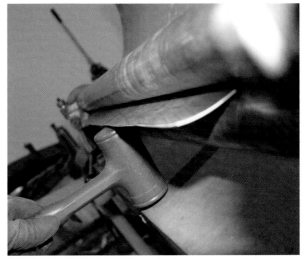

Once in the roll, the ends will warp and you may want to tap them into proper alignment before removing the metal. I use a rubber hammer for this.

Each floorboard (right and left) was cut out as a separate piece with the driveshaft well holding the two parts together. The rear section of each was also bent up 90 degrees to give the floor extra strength.

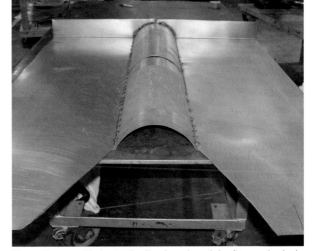

The well was welded onto the floorboards and the fit was checked again.

birthplaces of corrosion. A previous repair to the body, if not undercoated, can also lead to the start of rust.

Companies such as Evercoat, 3M, Por-15, Mar-Hyde and even some paint manufacturers offer products that help in the treatment and prevention of rust. If rust is a problem that you're dealing with, I recommend a visit to The Eastwood Company Web site. Eastwood offers both Evercoat and 3M products, as well as their own line of encapsulators, undercoatings and tools for the job.

Major Rust Repair

If you have any experience with body rot at all, you know one thing for sure: Rust is not your friend, or your car's either. A muscle car that might be worth $50,000 in very good condition might only bring a fraction of its worth on the trading block if any rust is present.

Proof that rust is a common automotive ailment can be found in the ad section of any car magazine. Dozens of aftermarket companies are making reproduction "patch panels" for most of the popular domestic and import models as well as vintage year classics.

What separates a minor rust repair from a major rust repair in my shop is the fabrication element. If the damage from rust is so severe that you can see through the panel, it's major! As luck would have it, I could find no such repro body parts for the '40 Ford, but there's a reason for everything. With my old rust bucket, I had the perfect patient to treat for major rust infection. Rust is a lot like cancer; if you don't get it all on your first attempt, it will come back to haunt you until you get it right.

Step one in repairing the '40's rotted out floorboards was to stock up on the right sheet metal. I went to my office and placed an order with my metal supplier, M&K Metals in Gardena, California, for two sheets of 18-gauge AK steel. And with the new metal on its way, I went out to the shop to cut out what was left of the factory floor.

The pan was flipped over and the seams welded from the bottom as well as the top.

Both sides of the front of the main floor pan hit the kick plates and had to be marked and trimmed down for clearance.

The front foot plates had to be fitted in place and it was again time to make patterns for the metal.

The old mounting bolts were in the way and had to be ground out of the way before a pattern would fit properly.

The right foot plate fit perfectly except in the corners, which had to be nipped off.

The next step was to make the transmission well cover.

If you are poor with layout and using bisecting lines, just lay paper on top of the trans cover and trace around the area where it meets the floor.

The trans cover is cut out and rolled for a test fit on the floor pan.

Once the pattern is removed, I have a trim line that will match the driveshaft well exactly. This is cut with a set of shears and the piece reinstalled for another fit.

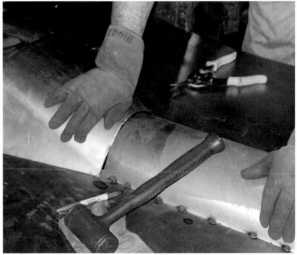

The part fits well enough to weld into place.

The same is done with the top trans cover. It is matched to the firewall and tack welded in place.

Since I planned some custom fabrication for the replacement of the rusted floors, I wasn't confined to cutting to the dimensions of a replacement panel. Basically, I had no limit on where to cut or where to stop cutting, except when I found solid metal. But the only solid metal near the old Ford that I could find was the car sitting next to it! So I proceeded to strip everything in and on the car including seats, carpet, and all the old rusted pieces that could be removed. I even removed the glass from the car as well as the door locks so I would not have to keep opening the doors each time they closed. The only remaining item inside the car was the steering wheel, which I left so that I could maneuver the car around the shop.

With plenty of space to work, it was time to make some patterns to use for cutting the sheet metal to proper fit. I use both cardboard and a clear pliable plastic called Vivak for all of my patterns because I can see through it and mark exactly along the edges that I need to cut or the places that require bending. As I laid them out, I marked them from

The pan is tack welded together and ready to be taken out and welded up for the final time.

The pan can now be welded and flipped for bottom welding without accidentally welding it to the car.

This is the last install of the floorboards in the '40. Now all I have to do is weld the new floor to the body, add a rust-proof coating and seal the seams.

Body Repair BasicsFor Customizing—Getting Off to a Smooth Start

Panel Replacement Tips

When you form a part such as a driveshaft tunnel, start along the centerline of the driveshaft well and shape the metal to fit over the driveshaft. Two things to consider are: 1) the spacing between the driveshaft and the underside of the panel, and 2) making sure that you create a flange that will go under the next floorboard so that the joint where the panels will be welded is double thick. When the tunnel is shaped and trimmed to fit perfectly, you can fit the next panel into place overlapping the wheel well flange.

Fabricating multiple panels requires that each one is put into place in order for the next one to be made. You can tack weld as you go along, but grinding tack welds each time you have to adjust or maneuver the pieces around during the trial fit can be a pain. Race car fabricators who do nothing but custom-fit body and interior panels use Cleco fasteners rather than tack welds. Cleco fasteners are sturdy, easily removable with a Cleco tool, and can be used over and over again.

As you progress with one panel after the other, the floor will start to take shape and before you know it, will look like a factory install. When cutting openings in the floor for a shifter or pedal linkage, remember to double panel that area for reinforcement. If beads are desired either for appearance or for strength, you will have to roll them into the completed panel with a bead roller before final installation.

The rust-damaged floor of the '40 Ford came together in one short weekend. Remember that floor seams do not have to be perfect if you plan to pad and carpet the interior, so don't knock yourself out on details here. When fabricating floor pans, the main concern is that they are strong and will support your weight. Don't forget to provide the necessary mounts for seats and safety belts.

To temporarily fasten metal in place we often use a tool called a Cleco fastener. The Clecos are like temporary pop rivets. All you have to do is drill a hole, about 1/8-inch, through both sheets of metal and put the Cleco in with the tool.

The Cleco tool looks like a set of pliers and simply compresses the end of the Cleco tip down in diameter until you slip it in the 1/8-inch hole and let the handle go. The tip then expands, grabbing the metal and holding it in place.

the front of the floor to the rear then marked each sheet with a letter and a reference to indicate its location and position with the adjoining sheet. This process took about two hours. After that I was ready for trimming to fit until I had floor panel patterns that were ready to transfer onto sheet metal.

The next step was to form a driveshaft tunnel that would traverse the interior from the firewall on back to the section directly over the rear end. The accompanying photos illustrate the remaining fabrication of the tunnel and floorboard.

Body Seams

The one and only reason why this subject is being broached here is that I've seen too many customizing jobs started on a car before the doors, fenders, hood and trunk are in proper alignment. The result is devastating for the customizer who perfectly radiused his door only to discover that it doesn't line up with the door post. Or one of the fender flares has an awkward tilt compared to the other three. So before you start any modification to the body, be absolutely sure that every panel is in proper alignment.

Does it seem like that hot rod or muscle car in your garage just won't look like the ones you see at the shows or in the magazine, no matter how perfect your paint job is? Is it possible that some cars just get so old that hoods

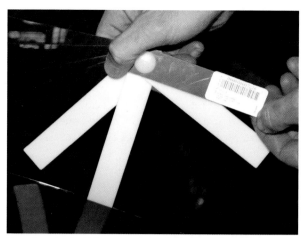

There is a plastic thickness gauge available through Eastwood Co. that can let you check the gap on doors, trunks and hoods, allowing you to adjust and center the panel to an exact distance.

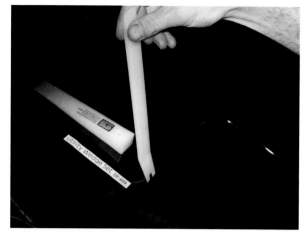

Plastic pry bars can be used to help move a painted panel without damaging the paint.

and doors and fenders won't align properly no matter how many adjustments you try to make?

Well, getting any vehicle to look as good or better than it did back when it was new requires more than smoothing out the body and laying on a perfect coat of paint. In order to achieve that show-quality look, each and every body seam, or gap, must be absolutely straight. But that's not all! The surfaces of adjoining panels must be level along the entire length of that seam where they meet.

Regardless of what type of vehicle we drive or how much of it we plan to modify or restore, you can't take it apart if you don't know how to put it together. So it's important to know some basic techniques that you can use to align the hood, the trunk, and everything in between.

You'll find that some body panels require no trick at all to replace. Others, say for instance a hood that was removed to swap an engine, can put an experienced body man to the test, especially if the hinges were loosened or removed and no reference marks were made to indicate the previous mounting point.

Whenever a car is involved in an accident, the damage oftentimes makes it impossible to simply replace a damaged panel with a new one. It's not uncommon to see a panel installed with a few of its bolts missing or an excessive amount of shims to compensate for a poorly repaired frame that doesn't measure up to spec. It doesn't take special training or expensive tools to align panels.

A perfect or near-perfect seam on a car is not something that makes you stop and say, "Hey buddy, nice gaps!" But if the alignment is off, the seams become very noticeable, especially if the car is painted with certain custom colors. As you become more familiar with this aspect of auto body repair before customizing, you'll soon develop a discerning eye for details. A few hours can make the difference between a pristine-looking car and a mediocre one. Panel alignment is an art and is more confusing than it is difficult. It requires a few inexpensive tools and a few hours, but can make a difference of thousands of dollars in the end value of your car.

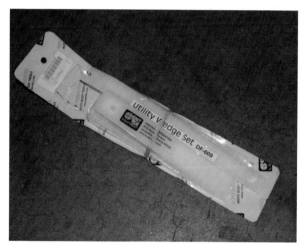

Packets of plastic wedges are also available from Eastwood that can be used for wedging a loosened panel into a required position as you adjust the panels and then retighten the bolts locking it down.

Adjusting Doors, Hoods, Fenders and Decklids

Before you start aligning a body panel, make sure that the full weight of the vehicle is on all four of the wheels. NEVER leave the car supported on jack stands during the process of body alignment because even the slightest degree of frame flex will throw your alignment off. A car can flex as much as 2 inches just by jacking the car from a corner of the frame. The second thing to remember before you start is to scribe a precise outline around the hinge brackets or mounting flange of the panel that you are aligning. This will give you a visual point of reference to make your adjustments.

Most hinges and mounting brackets are designed to be used with shims if necessary. Shims are thin washer-like spacers that can be used to bring a panel, hood or trunk into proper alignment. Shims are commonly used after a major collision repair. There are different types and sizes usually with a slotted hole so that the shim can be inserted without removing the entire panel assembly each time.

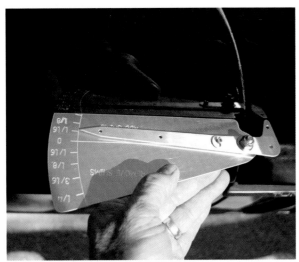

If you are adjusting the door hinge, you will need to put the alignment gauge at the door seam directly above the hinge. And there are two hinges so you will need to check the height at two points.

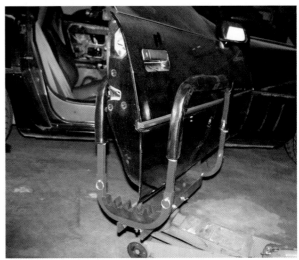

Eastwood also markets a door hanger or support that will hold the door in place as you adjust the hinges and is a great help if you are attempting the job alone. It fits most floor jacks so it can be easily lifted into place and adjusted with one hand.

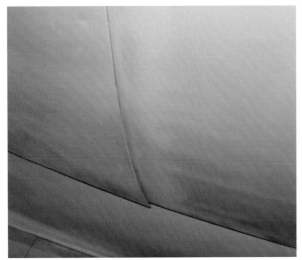

On older cars with overlapping doors the door will have to be adjusted by bending and body work.

Shims are cheap and you should have a small supply of them for body adjustments like this.

A good trick that helps me to align hoods, doors and decklids that do not need shims is to get the panel into place and snug up a few of the fastening bolts, but not too tight. Then I gently close the door, hood or deck and, with a pry tool, maneuver the panel into perfect alignment. The bolts should be snug enough to hold the panel in place, yet loose enough to allow movement. Once everything lines up, I install the remaining bolts and tighten them. If you're lucky, this will be enough to take care of the alignment.

Doors are simple to align if you have the right tools and the knowledge to use them. A door hanger is a great tool if you are working alone and need an extra hand. It adapts to most floor jacks and allows the weight of the door to be carried by the jack. To use it, you simply swap the lifting pad on the jack for the hanger and roll the jack under your door. Once the door hinge bolts are loose you can jack the door up to relieve the weight from the hinges and then juggle it into place. Never loosen all of the hinge bolts at

once. Loosen all but one of the door-to-hinge bolts and keep them snug. This will allow some degree of movement without flopping all around. You should not need to remove your hinges from the cowl unless the door is really out of alignment.

Door alignment can be frustrating and will task your nerves, so take it one step at a time and think in single directions of movements. First bring the door flush at the hinge area at the upper part of the door, then the lower hinge door area. After this, move to the seams and align the bottom of the door seam, then move to the front and rear seam and align them.

Let's say the door fits well but is a little too far forward. NEVER loosen top and bottom hinges and move it forward. Loosen the top hinge to the cowl/center post as described above and lift the rear of the door, a LITTLE. This will push the upper hinge forward. Now TIGHTEN that one bolt that was left snug. Do the same on the lower hinge, pushing down, but remember the weight of the door is helping, so little push is needed.

If the door fits well but is out at the top or the bottom, again, loosen ONE hinge to the DOOR in the manner described and push it out or in. If it is out or in at the top rear for instance, move the bottom front in the opposite direction. This will pivot the door on the striker, and move the rear top where you want. Moving the bottom rear takes moving the top front of course.

You may need to twist the door. If the front fits well and rear is out at the top (or bottom, just reverse) you can put a block of wood at the rear of the door and push in on the bottom to twist the door. Some will take a lot of force to bend, and be VERY careful not to let your fingers hang around the outside of the door edge. If you are hanging the door and you have access to the hinges, either through the wheel well with the skirt off or if the fender itself is off, you can simply hold the door up to the opening and push the latch shut. Then put the bolts in the hinge. The last step is to adjust the striker so the

This GTO has a few shims under the right trunk hinge that brought it into perfect alignment; the shims can be rotated out of sight but for the photo we left them exposed.

On this Mustang, as with many cars, the front fender can be adjusted by a few mounts, one of which is in the upper door jamb.

This is the shim gauge that I made for checking a flat surface and as you can see it even detects the slight curve in a roof panel.

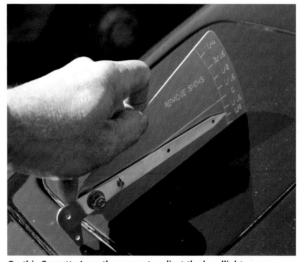

On this Corvette I use the gauge to adjust the headlight cover; these are always out of adjustment and easy to bring back with a little time and shimming.

door closes and latches freely.

Hoods are a special case for alignment as they are a large sheet of shaped metal or fiberglass that is suspended with a relatively weak point of leverage. This puts a lot of stress in the hood panel itself, as the hinges are spring-loaded or hydraulically dampened to control the raising and lowering of the hood. Many older cars and trucks have poorly designed hinge assemblies that tend to place the force of leverage in the center of the hood panel. To lessen the chance of warping the hood, be sure that these hinges are well lubricated and free to pivot at all points. Old Chevy trucks are famous for this "center hood buckling," and to make matters worse their hood panel is weak at the midpoint by design. So check the center return on the hood for cracks or tears in the metal or cracks in the fiberglass before an alignment continues. If damage is found it must be repaired first.

The best place to start on hood alignment is to first remove the hood latch mechanism to prevent unwanted locking of the hood. If the hood is too far out of alignment and is then latched it may be extremely difficult to unlatch. This unwanted latching can be prevented by simply removing the hood latch before alignment. Then, once the hood is in alignment, the latch can be replaced and adjusted. Even the hood latch can pull the hood out of alignment, so care must be taken when adjusting this as well.

When replacing the hood latch, use a piece of modeling clay or something similar and put it on the latch. This way you can see exactly where it hits on the striker. Bring the hood down till you just tap the clay but DON'T LATCH IT. This tells you where to move the latch.

If you have a hood where the hinges mount on the side of the inner fender well or the side of the firewall, "rotate" the hinge to make your adjustment. Just pushing the hinge up and down will give you very little movement on the top of the hood.

Another thing to keep in mind when aligning your hood: If you raise the back of the hood on the hinge or raise the back of the hinge on the fender, the hood will go up. If you raise the "front" of the back of the hood

Alignment Enlightenment!

The first step of panel alignment is to find out why you have a problem with the alignment. Are the door hinges worn out? Is a fender bolt missing? Did a body shim fall out? Or heaven forbid, do you have a bent frame? A door that is only slightly out of alignment may be difficult to latch or may not latch at all when you try to close it. A hood that is 4 degrees out of square may hit the fender, chipping the paint along the edge or worse yet, could jam shut requiring that you cut an access hole just to open it. The point being that alignment is critical and well worth learning to perform. It is either a result of poor assembly of the vehicle in the first place or the result of some type of accident. It could also be a result of a paint job where parts were removed for painting and not replaced correctly or just not aligned at all after assembly.

Any of the aforementioned evils can be the culprit of misaligned panels. If such is the case, you need only make the necessary repair and your alignment woes will be gone. In situations where a total readjustment of a door or other panel is required, you'll benefit from the use of a few specialty tools designed to ease the task.

- ◣ **PANEL ALIGNMENT GAUGE**—This handy tool is easy to use and takes the guesswork out of lining up your panels. It can detect as little as 1/64-inch difference in panel height to indicate how much to adjust or how many shims to add. The gauge will retain a measurement until you reset it and does not require any calibration. I designed and manufacture this tool for The Eastwood Company.
- ◣ **NON-MARRING PRY TOOL**—Making adjustments with a screwdriver or other metal object can damage paint and bend your panel. Specially shaped plastic pry tools such as Bojo's Auto-Tool or Dent-Fix wedges are a must here for minor adjusting.
- ◣ **A HEAVY-DUTY DOOR ALIGNMENT TOOL** such as Eastwood's Part Number 43674 should be used for more difficult aligning jobs. This handy device attaches to the door latch/striker assembly and requires a 1/4-inch breaker bar to make adjustments.

ON THE HINGE or the hinge to the fender, it will go down. Remember you are working with the *pivot point* of the hinge, not a stationary part. So if you loosen the front bolt on the hood, where it bolts to the hinge, and put a shim between the hood and hinge, this will LOWER the hood on that side. If you put that same shim under the rear bolt, it will RAISE the rear of the hood on that side. If you loosen the bolts from the hinge-to-fender and close the hood, the hinge will rotate down in the front. This will raise the REAR of the hood like putting a shim in the back bolt between the hinge and hood.

To lower the rear edge of the hood, loosen the bolts, only slightly, and LIFT UP on the front of the hood. This rotates the hinges downward at the rear, thus raising the front of the hinge and lowering the hood in the back. Remember to always leave one bolt on the hinge tight. If you want to rotate it back, leave the front bolt tight. If you want to rotate it forward, leave the rear bolt tight. When you move the hood forward or back on the hinge, leave the bolts snug enough that you have to tap on the edge of the hood to get it to move. Or if it needs to go back, leave the bolts a little snug, and wiggle the hood up and down and the weight of the hood will make it slide down. Remember, an adjustment only needs a 1/16 inch or so to make a 3/16 inch or more change at the front. To pull the hood forward

on the hinge, loosen the bolts so they are still a little snug so you have to pull up on the back of the hood to make it slide that little bit. If you loosen it up so it moves anywhere you want it, you will never know how much you moved it and you will move it too much, guaranteed!

Get the hood laying flat first, then move the hood forward or back on each side to make the hood fit the hole between the fenders. If the gap is large on the front right and small on the front left, then the hood needs to be moved back on the right side. As you move the hood back on a side it will close up the gap in the front of that side and open it at the rear of that side.

You may need to move fenders as well. Just do each change slowly, move it very little each time. Look at the bolt and washer as you move the panel. You will see where the washer used to be, and the amount is much easier to control if you watch the washer movement.

If you need to move the hood up or down at the front, you have a few ways to do it. First, on each side there are the "bumpers." The hood bumpers are located at each front corner and look like a bolt with a rubber pad on top. Just unlock the jam nut and raise or lower the "bolt" so it holds the hood at the height you need to match the fender. You may find that the hood won't go low enough even with the bumper down far enough. The latch may not be down far

The red Mustang in the back was one of my early custom Mustangs that made many covers and a few films. All the bodywork was in steel and the rear flares were our trademark for many years.

enough. When you close the hood, you shouldn't be able to pull up on the hood or push it down. The latch should be tight enough to hold it against the bumpers tight, but not too tight. If you have to apply too much force to open the hood or it opens with a loud "pop," the latch is probably too tight. If it is at the right height but you can lift it up some, then the latch needs to be moved down.

Aligning the trunk lid is similar to adjusting the hood, except that the hinges usually do not move. Therefore your only options beyond the movement in the slotted holes are shimming and twisting. If that's still not enough, then your only option may be to bend the hinge or the quarters. We recommend that you only do this if you have exhausted every other possibility.

Most of the tips for doors and the hood also apply to panels, with a few differences. Start with fitting the rear top of the fender. I like to put all the bolts in, loose enough so the fender can easily move. Close the door, and with the hood open adjust the gap at the top of the rear of the fender to door. After you tighten other bolts this cannot be modified so, do it first. Tighten the bolt under the hood closest to the door to secure the position. You may need to shim a bolt at the rear of the fender to the cowl to move the fender forward or back. After you have that bolt tight and the gap is to your liking, open the door and tighten the rear fender bolt that is at the top of the fender in the door jamb. Now do the bottom bolt, and with the door closed, adjust your gap. You may need to wedge a flat blade screwdriver or body spoon to "force" the fender forward to get the desired gap. Or just the opposite, use a 2 x 4 or something similar pushed against the front tire to force the

fender back to get the gap. This is one of the hard spots to get perfect because you have to get both the gap and the in and out of the fender to door at the same time with the same bolt. Some cars have two bolts that are far enough apart to get the gap and tighten the front bolt and then pull the fender in or out and tighten the rear bolt to get the flush fit of the panels.

Bending a panel is sometimes required. You can get this done in a number of ways. One is to use a block of wood. For example, let's say that along the edge of the hood there is a spot that is high but the front and the rear are perfect. You can lay a block of wood on the spot, right at the edge where it is strong. Using a big hammer—the bigger the better, trying to make a small hammer do the job can cause a lot of damage—hold the block and strike it nice and solid. Then check the results, you may need many strikes to do it. In doing this you may want to support the hood at the front with a block of wood underneath. This way the hood is up off the fender and it will bend easier because of the solid rest it has. You can also put the block under the edge of the hood at a low spot and, with steady pressure, bend it down at a point if you need it.

If you are working with very tight tolerances, you can actually grind the edge of a panel or jamb to get an extra fraction of an inch. Be VERY careful. Use a fine disk like 80 or 120. Take a LITTLE off. You don't want to grind the metal thin, of course, but a LITTLE can make a big difference when you are fighting for fractions. Here, you really won't be cutting too much metal, you are really just cleaning off all the primer and paint.

Chapter Three

Fabrication– The Art of Shaping Metal

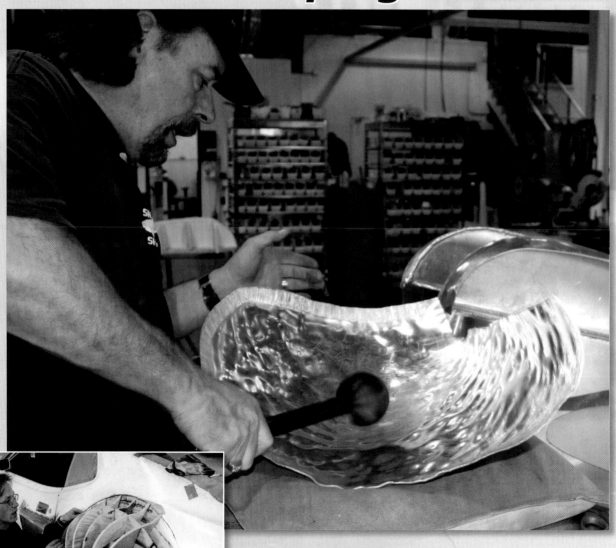

Mock It Up

If you've skipped the first two chapters in hopes of jumping right into fabrication, stop right here. Much of the basics that you'll need to know are covered in Chapter One. In this chapter, we're going to take everything that you've learned and, by example, try to apply it to making a part.

Production Line Fabrication: The Making of the Cars for the Movie "Taxi"

We sometimes build a mock-up part or parts that we can temporarily attach onto a car to show what the finished project will look like. Most of the times, the mock-ups we make in my shop wind up being used as plugs for vacuum-forming multiple parts for several cars like we did for building the stunt cars on the film *Taxi* starring Queen Latifa. The special taxi, if you saw the movie, was based on a late-model Ford Crown Victoria. The modifications were entirely cosmetic and included a full ground-effects body kit, front and rear spoilers, simulated fuel-injected supercharger protruding from the hood, and custom wheel covers. The outlandish performance of the taxi was the product of Hollywood special effects, but the actual parts on the car were not computer generated.

This particular job came from Fox Studios, which wanted seven identical taxis built with 12 extra sets of spoilers and ground effects all delivered to the studio in two weeks! There was only one problem—the studio had no clue what it wanted the finished taxi to look like. So I had a slight problem on my hands. The studio provided me with several illustrated renderings of what they wanted the taxi to look like from various angles, and although quite well drawn, none of the artwork was consistent from one drawing to the next. Basically, I had several drawings of different angles of different cars that I was supposed to make into one, times seven, in two weeks!

The side view of one car was not the same car that the front view showed. While the basic car was a Crown Vic, the art was basically a combination of concepts with different types and styles of spoilers, scoops and wings. It was as if the art director had no confirmation on any of the specifics, which I found out later was the case. I spoke to each person involved in the project at Fox to draw out as much information as I could and even invited the director down to the shop to have him describe what he had in mind. I could have just built what I wanted; after all I was the expert that they had hired to build the car in the first place. But having worked with the studios as many times as I have, I know that in cases like this, it's best to "never teach the pig to sing, it will waist your time and irritate the pig." So I suggest my way of doing it and then I do it their way, which they frequently change again and

The first meeting I had at Fox provided a chance to see the stock taxi that they wanted to morph into a hot rod cab.

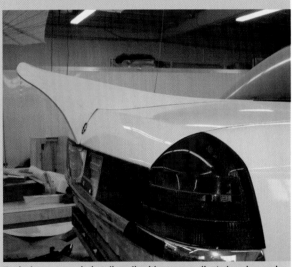

To design a rear whale tail spoiler (the rear spoiler/wing changed many times) we used a block of foam for a shape to decide how the profile would look and then tried to get an approval from someone at Fox.

One the design was agreed upon, we cut the outline for the tail on the band saw.

The mock-up of the rear spoiler consists of several wooden segments. Each piece is rough-cut at this point.

From the rear you can see how it develops into a finished design.

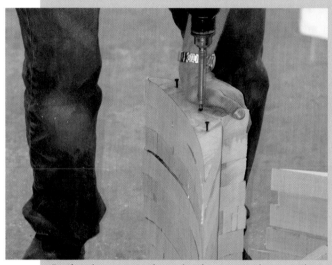

For the wing, we started screwing the separate pieces together for final shaping.

This wing design was set aside waiting for approval from Fox.

again until I'm up against an impossible deadline. This way they are happy and we make more money, so it's a winning situation for all.

So with only two weeks in which to build the cars, and no firm decisions in sight from the production company, I decided to make a mock-up that they could all look at. And when the inevitable changes would be ordered, I could accommodate them with relative ease since the mock up on the car would be constructed of wood.

When I make a mock-up of wood, I'm not talking about a flimsy, lightweight balsa wood framework of the design; I'm talking about solid wood parts that are shaped and sanded smooth down to the smallest detail. My reason for this is not just to promote the mass slaughter of a few good trees. It's just that even if we had final designs in hand at his time, which we did not, we would have solid wood "plugs" so that if, or when, they approved the design, my crew could proceed with vacuum-forming the real parts using the solid wood mock-up as "plugs." A plug is basically a sacrificial part made from an inexpensive material such as plaster, fiberglass or wood. A mold is cast around the plug, and then parts can be made from the mold.

Each plug starts with a system of laminating 2-inch-thick slabs of wood together to form the thickness required to fabricate a particular part. For instance, the front air dam consisted of 16-inch-thick wood at first. And as if on cue, the studio guys showed up and asked if we could cut it down by 2 inches. Later they had us add those 2 inches back on, then shorten it, and then lengthen it. Whatever they wanted, we did, and they paid for each change. But if I had made a thin

When complete, the bottom table moves out so you can remove the finished part from the table. This is called a semi-automatic machine.

We were getting the parts out at a rate of about one sheet per hour. Fiberglass would have resulted in about one part per day.

cheap plug, each change would have meant the previous plug would go in the trash and force us to make a whole new plug that would cost the studio a lot more money. So, by making it out of solid wood, we had a sturdy part that allowed us to cut off a section, then glue it back on, cut it off and glue it on, etc. etc.

It was at this point that we pulled the massive, and I might add heavy, plugs off the Crown Victoria and put them on our 4 x 8-foot vacuum-forming table and started mass-producing the body parts. We were pulling about 10 parts per day out of the machine; that's much more than we could have made with fiberglass and, at the end of the day, we weren't itching to death and covered with dust.

The seven cars were completed on time and the 12 extra sets of parts were delivered to the studio within days after that. This was an example of thinking ahead and making a solid mock-up that could also be used as a plug if needed. Even though working with wood might generate a lot of sawdust in the shop, it's a much cleaner mess than plaster or fiberglass, and the tools for woodworking are not that expensive. Body tools such as air sanders and grinders are all that you need. It does help to have a chainsaw and a circular saw, and a band saw and a planer... some glue... maybe a nail gun...

Many parts for cars such as ground effects, dashboards, consoles, door panels, and trim pieces can be vacuum-formed from plastic. We use the vacuum forming machine a lot in our shop and it is hard to think of not having it. Some other items that we vacuum form include battery trays under the hood (metal battery trays are prone to corrosion and rust, whereas plastic

After forming, the parts were cut out with saws or snips and set aside for paint.

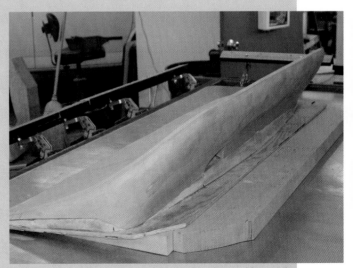

This rear area is referred to as negative draft and it would cause the plug to stick in the part. We were concerned about it and hoped it would not create too much of a problem.

The vacuum-formed spoiler fresh out of the machine is trimmed and filled with expanding foam to give it rigidity.

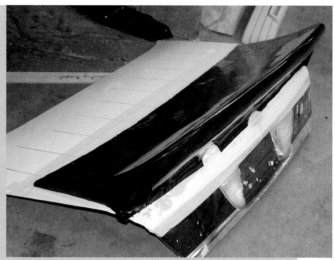

The first part came off the plug without much problem , but we used a thin sheet of 1/8-inch plastic. The final parts will be out of 1/4-inch ABS

A test fit to the car and we were ready to show it to the director.

This is the plug for the rear bumper area. I never said it was easy, just fast. This had to be made from slabs of pattern wood glued together and carved out. It weighed about 200 lbs.

This is the rear view of our car a few days later. All the parts were made on our vacuum-form machine.

will last for years), plastic headlight buckets and a glove box liner.

By now you might be wondering where to get a vacuum-forming machine and how much it costs. Vacuum-forming machines are fairly inexpensive and simple to use. The components of a machine include a heating element—which can be a portable shop heater—a vacuum pump and tank, and a perforated table top (similar to an air hockey table) that the pump is connected to by a plumbing pipe flange (floor flange). I've made my own vacuum-forming table by drilling a 1/2-inch hole in the center of a workbench to which I connected a valve and tank to it. Sure it's a bit more complicated than what I just described, but not much. If you're really interested in building one, there are a few good books on the subject, or you can pick up a used unit on eBay.

Even the hubcaps were made from plastic.

The supports were machined out of aluminum, but the wing (one of many designs) was PVC plastic.

When the "supercharger" was set down in the hood it didn't look half bad.

The rear door scoop was molded in and later changed to a Mustang scoop, but this shot shows the idea we were after.

I would not be without one. I have built many cars out of fiberglass and know the procedure well, but I have all but eliminated fiberglass from my shop. Plastic is the new-age material and fast becoming the way to custom-fabricate parts for cars.

Thermal plastic is the material used for vacuum forming. This means almost any plastic. The concept behind thermal plastic is simple and it is based on heat deformation. Heat it and it will conform to any shape; cool it and it will hold that shape. If you heat plastic enough it will deform, so if that plastic is heated around a form, it will take the shape of that form. A vacuum-forming machine simply streamlines the process.

Of the many plastics available, I use sheets of ABS for general forming of ground effects, headlight buckets and such. But if a special

At one point, the studio brought in an "air brush artist" to make the scoops look deeper.

Air brushing helped, but it was just a "trick" to fool the eyes.

Here, the artist shades and adds highlights that make the parts look real on camera.

The car, minus the hood, was ready for pickup by the studios again.

We made six of these cars and about 18 sets of parts for the stunts.

part requires any degree of strength, I use a polycarbonate such as Makrolon. I used Makrolon throughout the construction of the 10-foot mechanical great white shark that I built for The Discovery Channel's Shark Week special. Working with Makrolon requires a little more heat (longer exposure to the heating element) to form, but the end product is a very strong and shear-resistant plastic that can be drilled, tapped, machined or worked as if it were hardwood.

Wood Before Metal

I have worked with wood for many years and even built my own house along with most of the cabinets and furniture in it. The average car enthusiast may not realize it, but having a good working knowledge of wood really helps when it comes to customizing cars. Proper fabrication involves the wood mock up for a 3-D look at what you are about to build and for the actual fabrication process called "hammerforming." A hammerform is a wooden part used to hammer metal over to achieve a desired shape. Many hammerforms are used once, others can be saved and used many times. The building of a "buck" also requires good wood-working skills. A buck is similar to a hammerform in that it takes the shape of the object that you wish to fabricate. However, a buck is not used to hammerform. It's used as a guide to check your metal work as you fabricate. Special woodworking tools are also required to make a good pattern, plug or buck.

More Tools!!!

Woodworking tools are relatively inexpensive, but like any other tools, you should get the best-quality tools as you can afford. High-end tools hold their tolerance and have the power to cut through the thickest wood.

TABLE SAWS come in a variety of style and sizes from small hobby saws to fully professional saws, such as the JET saw we purchased for our shop, which doubles as a large work bench when not cutting wood for a project (always make sure that the blade is fully retracted after using the table saw!). I have always leaned toward a bigger tool than I think I need because I have found that once the initial investment is made for just a little more money you can almost double the quality of the tool, so "buy up not down" when purchasing the tools you need.

VERTICLE BAND SAWS are another great wood-cutting tool as you can make curve cuts with them as well as deep cuts in thick material. They start off where the table saw stops, allowing you to cut curves as tight as the blade will allow. If a buck for a custom hubcap is required, then the band saw is your tool of choice. JET makes a good tool at an affordable price. Another nice thing about a band saw is that you can buy metal cutting blades that allow you to cut sheet metal. If you do this, remember to slow the speed of the saw down or you will reduce the blade to scrap in seconds.

A good size band saw that can cut metal or wood is also a good investment as long as you have the room.

You will want a few wood tools if you are taking customizing seriously, and one is a good quality table saw.

This belt/disk sander works for wood and metal and will save you hours of hand sanding of small parts.

Spindle sanders are good for sanding a perfect radius on the inside of a curve. They have a set of different-diameter sanding spindles.

This large disk sander is great for squaring the end of a board. It's a little pricey, but nice to have.

DISK SANDERS are great for cleaning up the surface of the wood after the cuts are made or just for leveling the surface of an otherwise wave cut. If wood is laminated (glued onto each other to make it thicker), it can be sanded to level with a large disk sander.

PLANERS are good if you are laminating wood to make it bigger in any give dimension. For *Taxi* we ran each plank of pattern wood through the planer to ensure a constant thickness and a smooth, flat surface. This allowed us to glue multiple pieces together, making a thicker piece.

HAND-HELD ROUTERS are used with different cutters to make edges in the wood or to cut (route) out a hole in a piece of wood. We use them for making a consistent radius on an edge of the pattern as not many edges are square, but radiused for styling as well as strength.

TABLE FOR HAND-HELD ROUTER. This is the best way to use a router on a small piece of wood. You simply put the router in the router table, bolt it down to a workbench and pass the small piece of wood through the router. Keep in mind this is dangerous, so I would advise a class on woodworking if you like this idea. Many night schools offer such classes and they stress safety. I have many unpleasant router stories.

DRILL BITS for wood are different than drill bits for metal, so an assortment of them is in order. Keep your woodworking and metal working tools in separate boxes and never use one of the wrong material. Some metal working tools will work on wood, but not many. But I don't know of any woodworking tool that I use on metal.

WOOD GLUE is how you will be joining pieces of wood together. Try to stay away from using screws and nails as they will dull the cutters as you shape the wood. All you need is to be trimming an edge of a plug and hit a nail. Try to get in the habit of gluing all the wood together with either a fast wood glue or super glue with an accelerator to speed it up even more.

WOOD CLAMPS are inexpensive and you cannot have too many. They are good for holding the wood during laminating or just bonding the parts together during construction of a plug. There are corner clamps, strap clamps and pipe clamps allowing you to make the clamp as long as you need using plumbing pipe for the backbone of the clamp.

ORBITAL SANDER. This tool is good for smoothing compound curves as well as the straight flat areas and used when a part is too large or awkward to put in a disk sander. Just remember to keep the sander moving around as you sand, or you will sand in a "flat spot" on a compound curved area within seconds.

CHAINSAW. Not for the timid and not for finish work. It's great for mass removal of wood to get a large chunk in to a usable size in a very short time. We use them for sculpting things like stylized bodies on motorcycles and cars or on the occasional shark we have been know to create in the shop.

DISK GRINDERS are a lot like mini chainsaws for cutting away a lot of wood in short amount of time. The down side is that it will fill your shop with sawdust in just a few seconds, so try to take the grinding outside or have a ventilated area. Use a particle mask and a good-fitting set of goggles.

When working on wood, just think of it as reducing a block of wood to a finished piece. Another way to look at it is that the part you need is in that block of wood; all you have to do is find it and remove the rest of the wood around it. It is an art form, in progressive stages. The main stages are by quality of finishes as well, so the first stage is as follows;

ROUGH DIMENSION — Use a table saw, band saw or chainsaw to get the wood pattern or plug larger than the finish part by about an inch, but get it to look like what you want in shape and contour.

FINISH DIMENSION — This means bringing the dimensions to within a few hundredths of an inch, but make sure it is large by this dimension, not smaller. Remember to not cut too much away or you will have to ad more wood or filler and start this stage over.

FINISH SHAPE AND SURFACE — This is where the sanders and hand tools come in. This is the part that is the most time consuming and boring as you feel as if you are getting nowhere, but this is the most important stage, as it will determine the final parts finish. After the part is finished, you will need to prime or seal the wood to increase its life or finish.

You cannot have enough clamps. A set of C-clamps and other types should be around the shop.

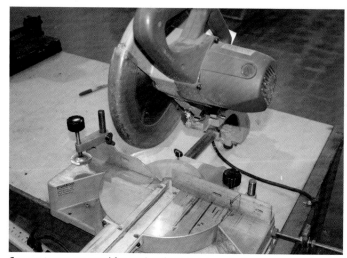

Cross-cut saws are good for cutting the wood down to the needed length.

While not a wood tool, an anvil is very handy for forming steel bars.

We often build bucks from wood to give us a guide to build the parts. On this '72 Mustang we are going for some real wide flares.

Good Wood Info

Always be aware that woodworking tools can quickly remove human body parts, a fact that my shop foreman can now attest to. Jon is the only guy in the shop who can only count to nine using his fingers due to a close encounter with a spinning chop saw blade. Have as much respect for woodworking tools as you do for your metal working tools.

Is all wood good for fabricating? Sometimes. There are two different types of wood that can be used for fabrication of molds and patterns: soft wood and hard wood. You will need to work with both, depending on how many times you plan to use your patterns and how intricate the part will be to form. If it is just a simple radius and not much hammering is required, then soft pine will work. Pine will most likely be the cheapest and easiest to find, however, common pine has a tendency to splinter and has a high moisture/sap content. Special pattern-making wood is the best to work with, but it will cost more. I use a wood called Jelutong, a low-density white wood imported from Malaysia. A special/exotic wood is expensive not only because of its fine texture, but also because of how it is prepared. Jelutong has the exceptional workability of soft wood with the strength of hard wood, is kiln-dried and usually stored in a heated warehouse to maintain a moisture content of less than 10 percent.

Heavy hammerforming will require a hard wood such as oak. But as the wood gets harder, so too, does its working properties. Hard woods require good-quality, sharp tools and long hours shaping and sanding to get a smooth surface. The smoother the surface the better the part will be. Keep in mind that any imperfections in the wood, or the hammer for that matter, will transfer on to the finished metal. Most people think that leaving a little flaw or two in the wood is not a big deal, but it can be. An example of what is known as "defect-amplification" can be seen when vacuum-forming a part from a wooden "plug." If the plug is the least bit dusty, the plastic will enlarge the imperfections about 100 times, making a dust speck look like a small pebble. Spend the extra time sanding down any blemishes in the wood before using it to back up a piece of metal.

This metal skirt for a 1950 Merc was made from steel off of a wooden hammerform. I made the patterns the same for both sides from one hammerform pattern.

We later tried to mount the skirts with a set of very strong magnets. It would have worked if we had more time to perfect the system.

Patterns

I cannot imagine building a custom car without having some experience in pattern making, or the ability to perform simple to complex woodwork. Much of what we do in the shop involves drawing, cutting, and taping of paper patterns to cars before we cut metal. In some cases we will build a complete part from solid wood to be used later for forming a 3-D shape. The "plug" allows us to place the metal on this shape and hammer the metal into the required form, then remove the wood with the metal formed to fit the intended area. This pre-wood part then gives you a spatial view of what the part will look like if you proceed with the intended design. Best of all it allows you to quickly and cheaply take it off the car and throw it away if you don't think it looks good on the car. Once you cut the car's body you are pretty much committed to the job and it will be very hard to reverse what you've done. So I highly recommend avoiding this headache by taking the time to collect some working knowledge of pattern making.

Pattern Materials

What is the best material to use for a pattern? Patterns are generally made of cardboard or paper, but sometimes thin polycarbonate plastic or Vivak is a better choice. My dad used to use real thin metal such as aluminum for his patterns so he could even go as far as shaping them once the basic outline was transferred to the proper gauge steel sheet. I prefer thin cardboard or, when I have it in stock, clear Vivak sheet of about 0.080-inch thickness. This material, made by Sheffield Plastic, has a lot of advantages because you can see through it for transferring lines or seams and it is relatively cheap. Best of all is that it will last forever and is waterproof. I cannot count the times I have dug out an old pattern just to find out that it has been ruined by water or moisture.

You can make patterns out of anything you want and you may even find a way or material that no one ever thought

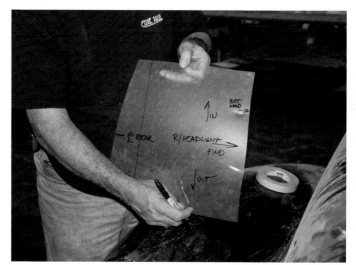

When making patterns, be sure to put as much information as you can on the material itself to help you correctly mark the steel.

Even a simple gas filler plug needs to be made from a pattern in order for it to fit perfectly, but the pattern can be made from plastic or cardboard.

The gas filler plug is a perfect fit thanks to good pattern making.

We decided to make an aluminum cover plate for the firewall of the '50 Merc, and the first step was to get general dimensions.

A rough pattern was cut from a large sheet of cardboard.

This cardboard pattern can be many pieces taped together.

of. But remember to stay open to other options and don't be afraid to mix and match your media. I sometimes use both wood and Vivak or cardboard and Vivak for my patterns so I can have a "window" to see under the cardboard.

Wire, paper, cardboard, metal, clay, plaster, and screen have all been used with some success. If you use a pattern you should use a material that defies compound bends, such as paper, cardboard or Vivak. If you use a screen material it can be pressed into a compound curve, as the metal can with some effort. But what you need is a flat pattern. I have used paper for the flat pattern and then transferred the shape to the metal, as well as a piece of screen, and then shaped the screen to give me a second 3-D pattern and save me from running back and forth to the car for rough fitting.

Tools for pattern making include drawing pens, pencils, paper straightedges and a set of "French curves" for laying out smooth curves, a large protractor is key for striking arcs, a tape measure, masking tape, scissors, a few razor blades, and an X-ACTO knife. A good quality cutting board will save your blades from constant dulling and, if you are making your pattern for wood or metal, then wood cutting saws and metal shears are in order.

A few things to consider:

- Paper is cheap, but not that strong, it is flammable and will sag if it gets wet.
- Cardboard is cheap and strong, it is flammable as well and will sag if it gets wet.
- Foam core is very easy to work with as well as it is easy to cut, it is stronger than cardboard and can take more moisture. It is more costly than just cardboard and is is a bit thick. I use the inside of the foam core as my reference, not the outside, as the 1/8-inch thickness on both ends (if you do a double bend) will add up to 1/4-inch increase.
- Plastic sheet (acrylic) is very brittle and will crack. It is waterproof and will allow you to see through it, but it will melt and burn if exposed to extreme heat.

Add small pieces to the pattern to fill in gaps by taping them on to the original pattern once it is in place. We used old business cards for filler pieces.

We then laid the pattern on a new piece of aluminum and traced the outline.

Cutting the aluminum can be accomplished in a number of ways. Here we are using an 18-gauge metal shear for the cut.

After a trial fit, a bead will be run around the part for looks and for strength.

◄ Plastic (Vivak) in thin sheets has the ability to withstand greater heat and it can be used for most patterns. It can be cut with scissors without splitting or cracking. Its down side is that it cannot be glued and must be taped or riveted in place. This is my all-time favorite material and the one I use the most because it can be bent, creased or dropped without damage and you can see through it. It comes with a clear covering that can be written on as you trace the pattern. If you fine tune your pattern you can rip the covering off one side and draw directly on the plastic.

◄ Wood is good but generally too thick for small stuff and will be hard to get an accurate pattern off of. It is used mostly for large sections of cars or for building a "buck" to work off of, where you need a semi-permanent mock-up that will last for an extended period of time.

◄ Thin sheet metal is more costly but great for a true feel of the finish panel. It can be shaped and bent just like

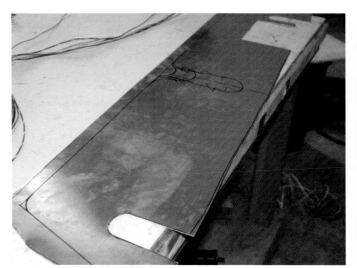

The felt tip marks are a guide on the aluminum for a bead design.

Fabrication–The Art of Shaping Metal

We had a bit of a clearance problem on the front end of this car and the only way to rectify the problem was to cut and lengthen the frame or slide back the fender opening, so we opted for the latter. This was accomplished by first making a pattern.

We had to make patches for some extra holes that were added to the front fender of this car by one of its many owners.

the real (proper gauge) metal that it is a pattern for. It can also be tack welded in place for set-ups. My dad used to irritate people by making his patterns of the same metal he was going to use for the car. Someone would tell him that he should use thinner metal for his pattern or cardboard and his response was "This is my pattern and my part. Once it fits I will weld it in." He had his pattern in his head.

➤ Screen can be used, but you have to be careful not to stretch it or you will get a faulty reading for a flat pattern.

A good pattern is like a working blueprint of the part that you're making. Like a blueprint, every pattern should be clearly marked to indicate its location and orientation (front, rear, left, right), bend points, etc. Some other important points on marking patterns are:

1. Do you plan to save your patterns? ID the part that the pattern is for; this is important and will help you if you ever make that part again. Keep the name simple like this: "1940 Ford headlight bezel."

2. What type of material do you intend to make the part out of once the pattern is complete?

3. Mark the pattern for left or right, unless it can be used for both by simply flipping it over.

4. If any special work is to be done on the finished part, mark it on the pattern, such as "bend this part up 65 degrees in or out (from the side the notes are on)" or "drill 2-inch hole on this center point". Mark bends with dashed lines and write next to the line "bend up" or "bend down" (or in and out) and how much to bend in degrees if possible.

5. Mark a centerline for the pattern if possible and as many notes as you need on the pattern to help you duplicate the part again if need be. I have added notes such as "this part is a pain to build, so take your time it can be done!"

6. If you are looking at, or working from, someone else's pattern and you see an X and a drawing showing an

angle with an X on one side of the bend, the X is an indication of the outside of the bend. It simply means that you will bend the part away from the X. This is something that was used years ago, and is still in use in a few shops today. You may develop your own method of making notes for bends and the other processes but try to write them for others to understand and make your notes clear and simple. Also write them so the notes will last. Using a waterproof marker would be a good idea. Also try a 3-D drawing of the part to show how and where the part will be bent, drilled and formed.

7. I draw an arrow pointing either forward or up and label it as such for a quick reference as to the orientation of the pattern. I then assume the markings are on the outside of the part so I know the orientation as far as in and out.

After you decide what pattern material you are going to use, you need to research your ideas for your project with photos and sketches. Start a project book in which you store all your ideas and sketches for the car project you are about to start on, clippings for magazines, scribbles on a napkin, drawings, and anything else that represents what you want to incorporate into your new car. This project book can contain a photo of a taillight, a scribble of a bodyline or a photo of a car with the color you want—anything that will document your ideas. It will be your memory bank and a way to show others what you want when it comes time for the collecting of parts.

Transferring the pattern information to the metal can be as simple as tracing around the pattern with a felt tip marker or a scribe, or you can spray a light coat of lacquer (white or black) around the edge of the pattern and lift the pattern off to see a stencil of the design on your metal. This works well on complicated patterns, but the old method of just marking around the pattern is the cleanest. Spraying will eradicate any notes you may need, but if it is a one-time pattern and you are sure you will never use it again, the spray paint works well and is fast.

A hammerform is just something that you hammer the metal over to shape the metal.

This project starts with the wood hammerform being made and the outline traced on the metal. Notice the pen spacer ring we have added for proper flange distance. This is a plastic ring attached to the felt tip marker.

How do you hold it all together as you add more parts to the pattern? Well, once you have the first part of the pattern, how do you attach it to the second part? I use duct tape, masking tape, rivets, super glue or bolts, depending on the pattern. In most cases I just tape the patterns together as I add extra parts. This may be a good time to mention that patterns should be made out of as many individual pieces as possible. Later, you can tape the separate pieces together to make one larger single piece.

It's a personal decision whether you should save your patterns or not. I could not count the times I have saved a pattern for years then thrown it out, just to need it a week later, so my recommendation is to save as many as you can as long as you can.

Hammerforming

For hammerforming, hardwood should be your choice of material. It will allow you not only to pound on it harder, but it will take more abuse than soft wood will without splitting and cracking. Keep in mind that the thickness of the metal will have to be subtracted from the surface of the wood. If the metal is to be added to the outside of the hammerform, the hammerform will have to be smaller than the part by the gauge of the metal. On the other hand, if the hammerform is to be used so the metal is pounded on the inside of the form, then the hammerform has to be larger by the gauge of the metal. Sound confusing? It is, but think of taking a hollow ball and wrapping a piece of clay around the outside surface of the ball. The clay will be much larger than the ball and will not fit into a hole that the ball would have fit into. I have no idea how many parts I have made off a pattern and forgot to allow for the thickness of the pattern material.

Once the hammerform is finished, clamp a piece of metal between it and another piece of wood, which should be cut to fit on top of the metal. This extra piece of wood is to hold the metal against the hammerform by a series of

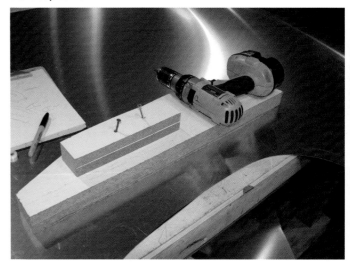

The forms were screwed together during the construction and now are separated and mounted on each side of the metal for the forming process.

The forms are clamped on each side of the metal in perfect alignment with each other. The purpose of this is to keep the metal flat during the shaping of the flange.

Tapping the edge with a soft hammer will bend the flange over the wood "hammerform" without warping the metal in between the flanges. Light taps are all you need and a few trips around the form should have the flange fitting the form perfectly.

When, the clamps get in the way, simply move them one at a time so you will have room to work on that part of the flange.

Just to the right you can see the finished flange. The clamp will have to be moved to get the rest of the flange bent. This flange can be a radius or a right angle as we are doing here, just make the shape in the wood you want the flange to follow.

Now the wood can be pulled out of the newly flanged metal and the part inspected.

clamps around its perimeter. Without this custom cut piece of wood the metal will just move around and buckle in the center. This backup board will now hold the sheet against the hammerform as you hammer its edges and stretch it into shape. Work slowly and use whatever you need to massage the metal into the areas that you want to go. You will have to remove and reinstall the clamps as you move around the edges of the sheet. This will allow you access to the edges while still holding the backup board in place and curtailing the buckling of the metal in the center.

It will take a bit of time and you will find not every shape can be performed on a hammerform, but many can and you will soon be making many parts you thought were impossible any other way. I have seen people make intake and exhaust manifolds, and also dashboards, on hammerforms. If you need a lot of side scoops for a certain car you could make a hammerform to mass produce them and have every one come out the same. On the side of my Mustang I wanted a scoop that would look somewhat like the old 1968 Shelby scoops and hammerforming was a good way to do this and get the consistency I wanted.

Now there are two types of forms that you can build for hammerforming: male and female. The male form requires that you bend the metal over a plug, stretching the outside of the metal to fit the shape. The female requires you stretch the flat area in the center of the part to allow the whole piece to stretch into the form. Which form to make depends entirely on your skill as a woodworker and a metal worker. But do not be afraid to switch from male to female if things are not working out the way you want.

Hammerforms are very handy to keep around our shop for common shapes that we will have to repeat often, such as outer and inner radiuses for corners. Hood scoops are another good project for hammerforming as well as headlight and taillight forms. This way we will have the same shape on both sides of the car. If you have a form made from wood, and you think it is a shape that you will be using a lot, you can have a local foundry cast an aluminum part for you. This

The finished part is a surround for a supercharger with the 1/4-inch flanges facing inward. Using a wood hammerform is almost the only way this can be done.

way it will probably outlast you.

A simple, but much used, hammerform is something used for radiusing holes in sheet metal for a cleaner appearance and a stronger shape. This is as easy as cutting a hole in a piece of hardwood about an inch larger than the hole in the metal, then radiusing the inside of the hole in the wood with a router and a 1/4-inch radiused bit. Make a backup board in the shape of a large washer. Its inside hole should be about 2 inches larger than the one in the bottom hammerform. With a series of small C-clamps, you can then align and clamp the hammerform in place and start shaping the edge down around the radiused edge of the wood with a small hammer or mallet. This will only take minutes and will give the hole a finished look that is hard to achieve any other way.

Hammerforms have been used for years in the automobile industry for the shaping of car bodies, and with a little practice you can master this very valuable skill.

Hammers and Dollies

The hammer and dolly are basic tools that every body man needs. There are so many different styles, types and kinds of both hammer and dollies that we could almost write a book on just that subject, and many of them are just copies of the basic style. Once you get down to hammer and dolly work you will settle down to just a few basic hammers and dollies. Over time you will find that almost

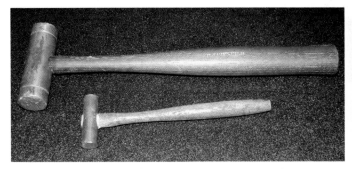

Brass hammers are for hitting steel without damaging it as much as a steel hammer will. They come in different sizes.

The swirled face of the hammer in the foreground indicates it is a shrinking hammer that grabs the metal and twists it together, thus shrinking it.

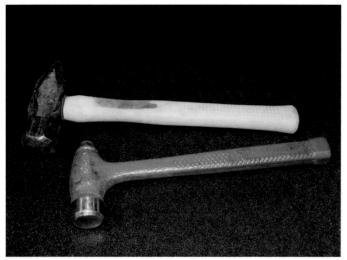

Heavy hammers are also very useful.

This shrinking hammer has a course face.

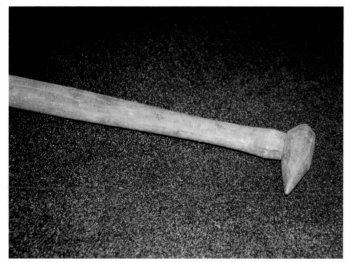

This small pick hammer is a real great tool for getting into small areas and picking metal either up or down.

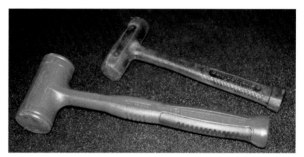

Rubber hammers are important because they move metal without stretching it as much as a steel hammer.

anything can be done with them by simple placement and combination of impacts. You can make metal do what you want it to do. You can shape, bend and form it into shapes you could only dream about. Learn to use the hammer dolly as well as you can because these are truly wonderful tools.

Body hammers are designed for just one thing, moving metal around by light blows against a sheet of metal. They are designed to fit into shallow creases and deep hollow spots, as well as wide-open areas. They are designed to transfer your swing into a movement of metal in any direction. A slight swing of the wrist and the metal moves a few thousands of an inch in the direction required to smooth out a rough spot or to align with an existing section of adjacent metal.

The dolly works hand and hand with the body hammer and, contrary to what many think, it is seldom used opposite of the hammer but off to one side of the hammer blows. That is to say that for most dent removal the dolly is held on a low spot and the hammer is tapped on the high spot close to, but not directly over the hammer. This way

you will get the benefit of two hits at one time—the hit from the hammer and the recoil from the dolly. I will go into this in more depth later in this chapter.

Dollies can be anything from a chunk of steel bar to a custom made and polished specialty dolly. Some of the types of dollies are as follows:

- A **toe dolly** is shaped somewhat like a big toe and used for general shaping.
- **Rubber-coated heel dollies** are as the name implies, this dolly though rare is sometimes used for shrinking, whereas a steel dolly will have the tendency to stretch metal if held opposite the hammer blow. The rubber allows for a bit of give that lets the metal move without decreasing its thickness.
- A **shot dolly** is basically a sand or shot bag that that can be hand held and used for shaping an area that cannot be removed from the car. I have often used them for moving a fender around by just hitting it with the shot bag as this will not dent the fender but imparts a lot of force against it. The shot bag will dissipate the weight of the bag over a large area so as not to dent the metal, but instead move the whole panel.
- A **heel dolly** is the same as the toe dolly, but used for areas that require a radiused edge.
- A **general-purpose** (GP) dolly is possibly the most used dolly in my box as it can be turned and rotated to get almost any shape needed.

This short-handled hammer was cut down for working in closer areas.

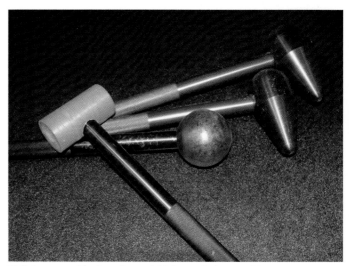

Mallets are good for bumping metal into rough shape and are normally made from wood or plastic. The hammer in the center is called a ball hammer.

➤ An anvil dolly is similar to the GP dolly, but has a full-radiused end protruding out one side.

I will not go into the use of each hammer because there is not a specific use for many of the following types or styles of hammers. It is an individual decision as to which hammer to use for which specific purpose. Some types of hammers:

➤ Wide-nose peen
➤ Door panel hammer
➤ Picking and dinging hammer
➤ Wide-nose cross peen hammer
➤ Cross-peen shrinking hammer
➤ Square-face shrinking hammer
➤ Long picking hammer
➤ Shrinking hammer
➤ Wide-face bumping hammer
➤ Reverse-curve light bumping hammer
➤ Short-curve cross-peen hammer
➤ Body hammer

When using a hammer and dolly I use a hammer-off technique most of the time. This simple method involves holding the dolly on a low spot and then hitting the high spot directly adjacent to the low spot. While holding the dolly against the metal you will notice that it will bounce away from the impact and if you are using force to hold it against the metal it will recoil back and strike the low spot from the underside, moving it upwards. This in effect moves the low spot up (dolly side) and the high spot down (hammer side) at the same time. With this method you are getting twice as much work done without stretching the metal. If you were to hold the dolly directly under the dent and hit the hammer on the metal in that spot the metal would be compressed between the hammer and dolly and the metal would decrease in thickness. This would force the metal into the surrounding area, thus stretching it. If this were to happen you would then have an "oilcan" condition and need to shrink the metal back into its previous shape to get rid of the stretched area.

Different hammers do different things and you'll probably want an assortment of them. Pick hammers are good for getting into tight spots to either raise, if hit from below, or lower if hit from above, a small spot. They can also be used to shrink an area by picking small pimples in the metal that will "draw" the surrounding area inward toward the picks.

High crown hammers are for concentrating the energy of the hit to a smaller area of the face of the hammer, whereas a flat hammer will spread the load out over the entire face of the hammer. Flat hammers will have less of a tendency to stretch the metal than the high crown hammers do.

Picks are used to "pick" up a small area or to remove a sharp crease when the area is too small to use a conventional hammer.

Slapping dollies or spoon dollies are placed between the hammer and the metal and can be used for everything from prying a dent out to spreading the impact from a hammer blow. Some slapping dollies act as hammers and are used by themselves as a means of working out slight high areas.

Sand and shot bags are another tool you will want if you are planning on shaping metal off the car, for example a patch panel situation. And then you will need a set of plastic or rawhide mallets … and … well, you get the picture.

It never ends. You will always need and want more tools. But what the heck, you bought this book, so suck it up and buy some tools. You want to build car or what?

So back to the sand bag and mallets, you will need two leather bags one filled with sand and the other filled with a No. 8 lead shot. Then you will need some soft plastic or rawhide mallets, I have a mallet I have designed that we call a ball mallet. We make them in three different sizes and they are perfect for shaping metal.

The biggest trick is to relax and enjoy shaping the metal. Keep in mind that the piece of metal that you're shaping is worth only a few dollars, so if it doesn't come out right, throw it away and start over. If it turns out perfect, then it's priceless! So have fun and experiment with the bag and

A spoon can be used like a hammer if you need to take a high spot down or spread the force of a hammer blow over a larger area. This can be done by simply placing the spoon between the high spot in the metal and the hammer.

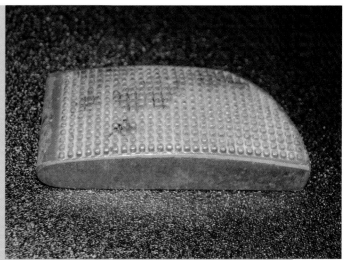

A shrinking dolly has a grid pattern on the surface. The idea is that the metal will be pressed into the surface and in the process "shrink" toward the dolly.

They look like the heel of a shoe and are called heel dollies. The one on the left is rubber coated for shrinking and the steel one on the right is for shaping.

Two dollies come in different sizes and are used for backing metal in strange contours.

Special Dollies

"T" dollies have been around for a while and no one knows for sure who invented them, but they are little more than a round bar or metal welded onto a flat bar. The round bar is designed to have a full radius on each end. The flat bar that is welded midway is out there as a means of clamping it in a vice. The full radius on both ends seems a bit redundant to me so I invented a P dolly with one end flat and the other end radiused. This way you have more surfaces to shape with. Plus, I added a set of three grooves to the flat end so you could work out imperfections in beads or sharp radiuses or even bend bar or tubing over the bar for matching required radiuses. We use these all the time and it is rare to not see one of them in the vice at all times being used to shape something. I have a complete set of them in diameters of 1/4 inch to 4 inch.

Almost every panel on a car has some type of radius and many parts have compound radiuses so the P dollies are one of the most used tools in our shop. We even have unique square and rectangular dollies for special occasions. I once made a dolly just for shaping the ends of louvers after rolling them. That's right, we "roll louvers." We made a louver roller die for our bead rolling machine and we roll our own louvers so we are not limited on the length or shape of them as you are with a louver press. We use the louver dolly to reshape and sharpen the end radius.

mallet and you will soon know just where and how to hit the metal and it will become second nature in no time.

Forming Small Parts With a Press or Roller

Designs or logos can be cut from wood or metal and rolled or pressed into sheet metal or sheet aluminum without a lot of work. You can simply take a saber saw or scroll saw and cut a set of flames out of a piece of hardwood or even plywood and separate the two pieces (the flames and the outer part the flames were cut out of) then place a small sheet of soft aluminum (3000 series) between them, set the composite on the ground and drive over the stack. Now separate the stack and look at the resulting sheet of aluminum.

This was a very quick example using a car instead of a press just to show you an example of what can be done with a simple arbor press or set of steel rollers. The smaller the part, the less pressure it will take; the more concentrated the pressure, the more pressure you can exert with what you have available. For a very small design, you can use thin sheet metal between two sheets of 1/4-inch steel that have been cut out on a male/female die using a plasma cutter and a grinder to shape the edges. Then, if the design is small enough, a shop vise could be your press. This method can produce small logos for hubcaps or pieces to weld into larger sheet of steel, adding detail you could not add otherwise.

Planishing Hammer

The planishing hammer and English wheel are two tools that look somewhat alike and are often confused with each other. Of the two, the most commonly used is the English wheel. It is ideal for rolling a sheet of steel or aluminum into a particular shape, such as for a fender or motorcycle gas tank. But the hammer has its applications which differ from the wheel in very distinct ways.

Since the planishing hammer is one of the tools that I designed and now manufacture for The Eastwood Company, I'm able to let you in on a little secret: The planishing hammer is little more than a pneumatic rivet gun with a hammer head installed and mounted on a "C"-shaped frame with a radiused anvil mounted opposite the hammer head. The term "planishing" means to smooth up metal with gentle hammering. The concept is that the heads of the hammer and anvil will both lower the high spots and raise the low spots simultaneously as the metal is fed between them.

Planishing hammers are making a strong comeback thanks to the many "build" shows that have saturated cable TV. It seems as if a workshop is not complete without a planishing hammer and English wheel, and this is one of the main reasons that I designed a set of these tools that the average person can afford. A planishing hammer is used

When Imperfect Is Perfect

Imperfections have a way of creeping into the metal without really trying to put them there so you'll have to make an extra effort to avoid them. But there are exceptions. My dad used to make "antique" lanterns, and to "age" the metal he would roll the new sheet of copper through a defective set of rollers. He found that by damaging the rollers on purpose which involved grinding them and welding near them and allowing weld splatter to stick to them, they would age, and any metal fed or rolled through them would look as if it had been kicking around the shop for 50 years.

He noticed that it did not take a lot of defects to really "age" a new sheet of copper.

We build English wheels and planishing hammers mounted on a universal tool stand.

more for smaller areas and raising a bump or scoop in the center of a panel, while the English wheel is for reshaping a whole panel. Both tools can almost always be interchanged with the same results, but there are times when a planishing hammer will work better or faster. I sometimes use the planishing hammer with a set of damaged dies to distress a piece of metal, making it appear aged by passing it through the dies a few times at random speed and direction. It works like nothing else to give a random pattern of flaws to an otherwise perfect sheet of metal. I used to use a pneumatic hammer by hand against a sandbag to shape scoops on cars,

After a panel is pounded out "roughly" on a sand bag it needs to be wheeled into a smoother finish.

and this worked fairly well, but it does not compare to the planishing hammer mounted on a stand. The stand mount keeps both your hands free for holding the metal as you hammer. The dies, which can be custom made for special jobs, will determine the final radius of the shape.

The combination of a hammer and a wheel is an unbeatable duo for the garage or small shop. A fun project you may want to try that will get you used to the hammer is to make some medieval armor, like a helmet, breastplate or even a shield. That kind of stuff is fun to make and will also dress up your shop with a piece of art that your friends can see and when they ask who made it, you can proudly say "I made that, just for fun!"

English Wheel

Metal can be shaped in many different ways. Some methods involve single bends, some involve more difficult compound bends in which the metal is bent in two different directions at the same time, creating a convex or concave shape. Older automotive fenders such as our 1940 Ford are prime examples of the compound curve. The compound curves provide an enhanced appearance with smooth flowing lines and the metal has more strength, due in part to the shape and the fact the metal has been work hardened.

Wheeling takes some time and you should be as comfortable as possible, so find a chair of the proper height and take your time.

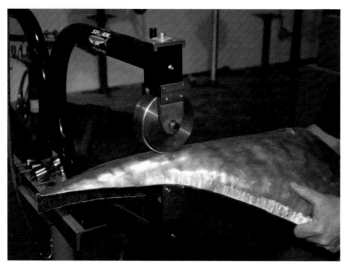

For a highly contoured shape such as a tank, you may have to change anvils to accomodate the various curves.

This gas tank half for a motorcycle took about 20 minutes to wheel smooth.

An English wheel and a few supplementary tools to rough the metal into shape are all you really need to make compound bends. These tools include a sandbag, a few shaping hammers, a shrinker and a stretcher. If you follow along with the accompanying photos, we will try to cover the basic concept of shaping metal with a few exercises that will show the principles of the English wheel.

We will start with some 12-inch squares of 3003-H14, half-hard aluminum, 0.063 inches thick. You can wheel either steel or aluminum but we are using aluminum in this example for its ease of shaping and its ability to anneal with a simple torch. On most cars you will be shaping steel and the process is essentially the same, but aluminum is good for practice.

Many people get the English wheel and the planishing hammer confused with each other, and for good reason. The biggest difference is that the planishing hammer allows you to work smaller areas than the English wheel does and the hammer is an air-powered tool. Like a planishing hammer, the English wheel can be used for smoothing out a small wrinkle in a panel or creating a curve or raised section in a piece of metal (aluminum or steel). Where the English wheel excels is in working with larger panels, either adding contour or smoothing welds or slight imperfections. It is the perfect tool to follow up a mallet and sandbag to help smooth out the rough shaping of a part. These two tools will turn the average hobby workshop into a professional metal worker's shop.

English wheels come in a variety of sizes, but for the weekend fabricator, I recommend a smaller benchtop size. One of the handiest wheels is the one that I designed for The Eastwood Company. It's large enough to handle most jobs yet small enough to fit on a workbench to make anything from hood scoops, fender skirts, motorcycle fenders or even a motorcycle gas tank. One thing that sets my version of the tool apart from others is that it can be ordered as a set with a planishing hammer. Together, these tools will enable you to customize almost any part of a car body.

English Wheel Techniques

This English wheel frame is constructed from sturdy 2-inch mild steel tubing that is mandrel-bent into a gentle curve, allowing space for your work piece due to the 22-inch throat depth. We have also included three of the most common anvil wheels, ranging from flat to medium crown. The solid steel rollers are fitted with bronze bearings for trouble-free extended operation. The wheel is also designed to be portable and easy to set up, so it can be stored away after each use if necessary.

The most unique feature of the tool that I designed is that it is convertible! This is the only tool on the market that can be converted from an English wheel into a planishing hammer within minutes utilizing the same frame. An English wheel's value, like most metal-working tools, improves with operator experience. I suggest that you practice on clean scrap metal before working on your project.

The English wheel frame should be securely mounted at a comfortable height to work with. We have found that instead of standing while using the tool, it's nice to use a rolling stool to help keep the metal at a comfortable working height. This is a personal choice and there is no one correct height for all people, so try different heights until you find the one that is comfortable for you.

The tool can also be bolted to a workbench. If a pedestal stand is used, it must be bolted to the floor to keep the wheel from walking away because of the pushing and pulling of the metal being shaped. We have also designed a channel that will hold both the planishing hammer and English wheel on a common stand. This channel also holds the extra wheels and anvils.

Keep the area clean and neat.

Keeping the work are neat and clean is important. Many times during large movie projects we all stop for "clean up time." It is a chance to organize and relocate your tools while putting away the tools you don't need. An organized area is much more conducive to productivity and a better-looking, finished project.

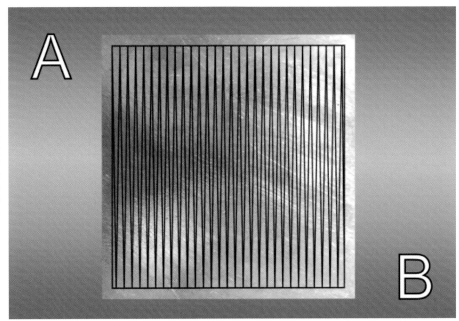

This illustration shows a simple pattern for your English wheel that should provide you with a compound curve on a flat sheet of metal. This is the motion that should be practiced to give you the hand control over the direction you want the sheet of metal to travel through the wheels.

Keep the metal clean and deburred.

Having clean metal is crucial. It does more than make you look professional, it makes you professional. Constantly wiping the metal and wheels down will eliminate marring from dirt or other foreign objects getting between the wheel and metal leaving imperfections on the finished work. A single piece of dirt on one of the wheels can leave hundreds of indentations in a sheet of metal before it is discovered. Get in the habit of wiping down the wheels.

Keep checking your progress against the form or project.

Wheel lightly and check often so you don't over-shape an area. Constantly check for fit on the metal and get in the habit of guessing how much wheeling will produce a particular amount of curve. Wheeling is about 80 percent skill and 20 percent muscle. Success comes from getting a "feel" for the tool and the metal.

Less is better than more.

It is easy to over-wheel a part, rendering it scrap or at least more difficult to repair. Less is better than more when wheeling, so take light rolls not heavy rolls. It seems that turning the bottom wheel tighter will save time, but it will only crease the metal, giving you more work. Take it easy and don't overdo it.

Slow your roll to acquire the skill.

Another skill that will come with time is the art of moving the metal back and forth and turning it just the right direction and just the right amount for the reverse run. The best way to gain this skill is to start out very slowly and get the motion down as you increase you speed. This will take practice, but it will become second nature with time.

Mark the metal to show how to roll.

Don't be afraid to mark the metal as to where you want to roll a high crown and where you want a reverse crown (this should be marked on the backside of the

sheet). After you roll the sheet and check it, wipe it down to remove the marks and remark it as needed. This will help you keep track of the progress.

Change the roller to change the curve.

Our company sells a tool that will help you figure out which bottom wheel you need to match a curve. This tool is to be used as a reference only and is not an exact template The curve or shape can be changed if you under-roll or over-roll an area. But the template will help get you the general shape you need, the rest is up to you.

Practice with aluminum.

It is the easiest metal to work with and will teach you the basics with less effort than steel. Later, you can apply your newly learned skill on auto body sheet metal. The best alloy of aluminum is 3003 H14, half-hard aluminum 0.063 inches thick. Other alloys can be used, but this grade is the best for welding and working.

Keep the metal dry or it will attract dust and dirt.

With every move of the English wheel, the metal is stretched a little bit over the lower wheel crown, creating the curved shape. Therefore, the more curve there is in the lower wheels, the more curve you add to the metal being shaped. The flatter the crown of a lower wheel equals less curve. Try not to over-work an area. Removing a high crown is not as easy as putting one in. Work slowly and double-check your progress often, especially if you are making a body panel.

Basic tracking.

The usual grip on metal being shaped is thumb on top, hands at both sides in a position near the rear of the panel if shaping a smaller part. If shaping a larger part, your hands should be near the center or point of balance.

There are three points of entry for inserting the metal panel between the wheels: front, side and open. The frontal entry method is used when you already have a set wheel pressure that you do not want to change. Simply place the metal to be shaped between the two wheels and push forward slowly but firmly and don't force it. Too much pressure and you might ruin the metal by crumpling or folding it. Entering from the side with a pre-determined pressure on the wheels is ideal when working on spots near the edge of the metal. Set the metal alongside the wheels at a slight angle. As the metal enters you will feel the wheels take hold. Continue for 1/2-inch into the metal, or to the problem area and straighten the piece so it runs parallel to the wheels. Further tracking will stretch the edge.

The open method is the most common entry. With the wheels adjusted far enough apart to insert the sheet of metal, place the metal with the position to be worked between the wheels. Now add pressure and begin working the metal. This method is also ideal when an area to be worked is located towards the middle of a panel.

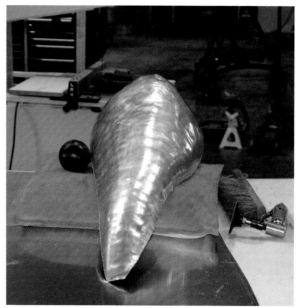

A project can bounce from the wheel to the sandbag and back many times before it's finished.

We'll start with a basic example. The ideal tracking path is a series of tight zigzags spaced about 3/8-inch apart. Start at one corner and slowly work the metal back and forth until you reach the end. Now try going in reverse of the pattern you made by tracking the metal back to the starting point using the same zigzag pattern.

Cross-wheeling the metal is exactly as we described earlier, but with the piece turned 90 degrees. This is the essence of shaping with the English wheel. You should refrain from rotating the metal being shaped while between the wheels as they will mark up your work.

If all the tracks in a tracking pattern end up on the same line, the effect is very noticeable. Instead of a smooth blend from one shape to another, there is an abrupt transition. This can be dealt with by the "staggered stop" method. This technique uses two different stop points for the track lines as can be seen on the example. Note the alternation of the stops between different tracks as the metal is shaped, and is done during the 90-degree cross-wheeling as well. This method blends the newly raised metal and the old shape much smoother, producing better results. On some larger projects you may have three or more stop points in order to create the desired shape.

The previous examples show how to raise the metal. Now let's look at a way to remove the raised effect. Using the same light pressure as before, enter the metal into the wheels from one side. Track along the edge three times, then inboard for 1 1/2 inches using the 3/8-inch tracking method as indicated in the example. When reaching the end of the pass, track back outboard, omitting the edge tracking.

Treating all four edges this way removes much of the shape that was raised by the earlier examples. If the shape

has not lessened much, try increasing the pressure a little and try again. Should your pressure be too high, the edge will take on a wavy appearance during the edge tracking. If this happens, concentrate on the inboard tracking until you have a flat edge again. If too much of the raised shape remains, try the same technique as before, but go inboard for 3 1/2 inches on all four sides.

Sometimes you will have a "soft spot" in the metal being shaped. This is detected as a slight oil can effect in your metal. When you press on the "soft spot" it will click from the front to the back side each time it is pressed. To remove imperfections like this, find the edge of the affected area and mark it with a pencil or non-permanent pen. Its position on the metal, either on the edge or in the middle, will determine how many and where the passes should be.

The accompanying examples illustrate a few different tracking paths that can be used to remove a soft spot. Note the tracking pattern has a variation; the tracks are opened up at the end of each pass, instead of the usual 3/8-inch pattern. This serves the same purpose as the "staggered stop" technique discussed earlier, which blends the new shape into the old. Also note that the passes are not required to be parallel to the edges. They can be any direction that serves the purpose at that time. Using a light wheel pressure begin tracking next to the problem area, then away from it.

Repairing a wavy, or loose, edge requires a similar technique. Mark the area and begin tracking the edge. You should only track the length of the loose edge and not the entire length of the metal being shaped. Remember to open up your tracking as the pass ends.

The remaining chapters is this book are basically a compilation of modifications that my crew and I have performed on various projects at Customs By Eddie Paul. You can select any one of them to try, or you can combine several to achieve a particular look for your vehicle. Good luck!

Chapter Four

Customizing Techniques—
A New Look at Traditional
Custom Bodywork

Many years ago we built this little '66 'Stang that graced the covers of many a magazine, and was in a few shows as well. It was my daily driver and ran as fast as it looked.

The first steps in a sunken antenna project are figuring out how many you want and where you want them to go. Then do a fast check to see if you have enough room to put them in the desired spots with the allowance for the sunken tube of about 4 inches. Marking them with tape allows you to move them easily.

I never thought I would be making washers, but this was the fastest way to get the dimension to plug the bottom of each antenna tube. I used a step drill for this and will trim the outside off later.

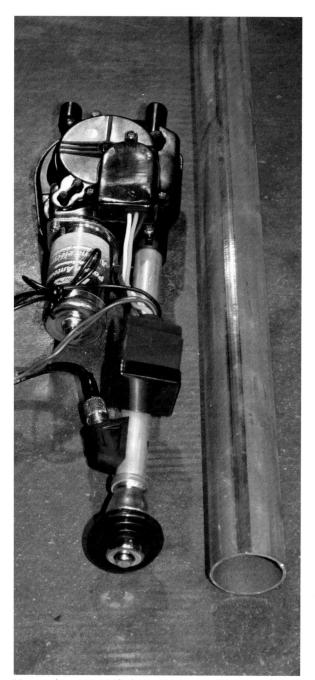

Measure the antenna to find out what diameter tube you will need to stick the antenna into. I found that a 1 1/8-inch seamless tube works well. Be sure it is seamless or you will have to get the seam ground down smooth later.

The Sunken Antenna: Your First Customizing Project

I highly recommend that you start your customizing career off with a small project. If you've learned about metals and basic welding techniques in the previous chapters, you are ready to sink your power antenna. This is one of the easiest projects for a beginner and one with big rewards for style and practicality. A sunken power antenna provides a stylish recess that hides the entire base of the antenna when it is fully retracted. When the mast is raised, it will appear as if it rises out of nowhere. This is a small modification,

but will change the appearance of a vehicle drastically by hiding what is an otherwise ugly attachment to any car.

A power antenna is not an absolute requirement for this modification. The sunken antenna trick originated long before the power antenna so don't feel limited to power units only. In fact, if clearance limitations are what's holding you back, a standard manual antenna may be the best solution.

But before you start, there are some practical points to consider regardless of whether your antenna will be powered. First, a sunken antenna will definitely create a water trap, so you will need to incorporate a water drain with a somewhat direct path for the water to drain or be able to attach a hose

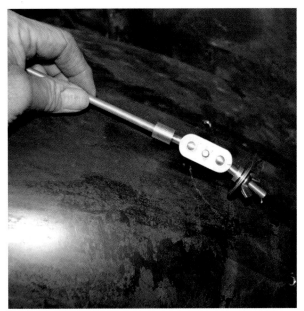

This tool is the prototype which I built for this installation. It has since been revised and simplified and is sold in a kit. Both versions have a threaded stud base that fits through the 1/4-inch hole drilled in the fender and are firmly attached to the fender with a wing nut.

On this prototype the base has a bar that has to be set level vertically with the ground. On the newer model we supply a bubble level that is much simpler to use.

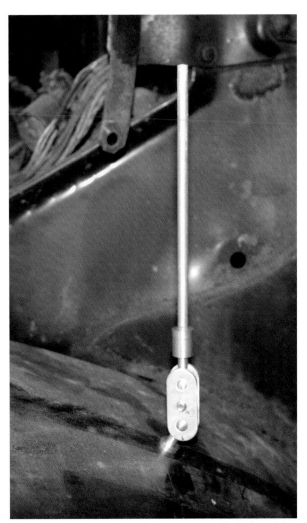

This base is then aligned or leveled so it is perpendicular (at a right angle) to the ground. This will guarantee a professional job as you install the tubes in the fender.

The laser holder is then added — it is nothing more that a laser pen that will shine a laser light dot onto the fender. As it is rotated it forms a perfect circle on an irregular surface. This beam of light can be traced with a marker to give you the pattern to cut out.

to the drain to route the water elsewhere. Second are the issues of clearance for the antenna base mechanism (which is much larger on power models), clearance for the mast as it travels up and down, and routing of the antenna cable. Finally comes the question of where it will look good on the car. Once you have these things worked out, you are ready to start.

To begin with, you'll have to select the antenna that you want to use on your car. Most universal-fit power antennas will work for this modification; we used an off-the-shelf unit from Napa Auto Parts. Most people will probably opt

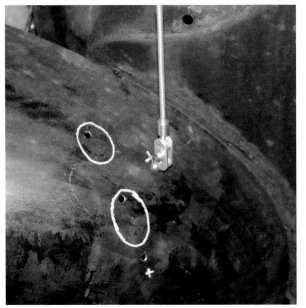

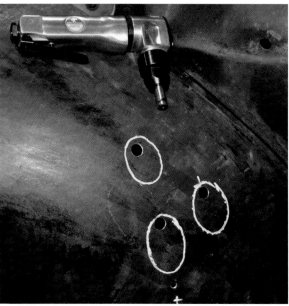

Two holes marked and the third ready to mark. The hole near the bottom was not used and later welded up, but it was a possible location for the third antenna.

The nibbler was used for cutting the holes out. Do not try to use this tool for a finish cut, it will leave rough edges.

For roughing out the hole, I use a pneumatic nibbler which takes about a 1/4-inch hole to allow it to be inserted into the metal to start cutting the hole.

for installing just one sunken antenna, but you can do two or as many as three of them if you so choose. I chose to sink three antennas into the left front fender of the '40 for no other reason than I feel things look good in multiples of three. This is a personal preference, of course, but the methods here will apply to the installation of any number of antennas.

After determining the best location to sink the antenna—an area that looks good and provides adequate clearance for both the antenna tube that you'll be making and the antenna mechanism—you'll have to mark the spot on the car where

These are the homemade washers for the ends of the tubes we cut earlier. The outsides do not have to be perfect as they will be welded all around and ground down when finished.

A test piece of the same tubing was used to check the holes for fit. Don't expect them to fit the first time. Most of the time it will take some grinding to make them fit.

We used a die grinder for fine tuning the holes to the proper shape. Be sure to wear goggles.

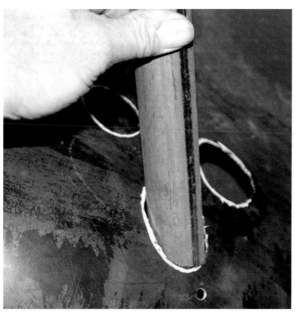

When you are satisfied that everything fits, it is almost time to start welding the tubes in.

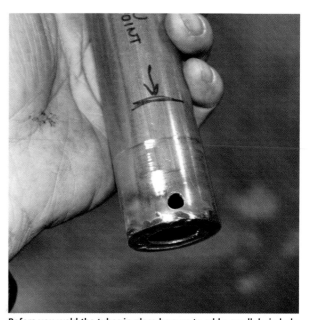

Before you weld the tubes in place be sure to add a small drain hole to the bottom of each tube to drain the water that collects in the tubes during rain or washing your car. Also, mark about 4 inches down from the capped end for a depth reference when installing the tube in the fender.

the antenna will be sunken. In order to accomplish this, you will need to know the diameter of the tube that you'll be using. Aesthetically, the smallest tube diameter that you can use is usually the best. The minimum tube diameter is determined by the size of the antenna's retaining lock nut, which must be inserted into the tube. In the past, I've used old discarded shock absorber housings for this or simply found a piece of scrap steel tubing about 12 inches in length.

Once you know what tube diameter you'll be using (I used a tube size of 1 1/2 inches O.D. on the Ford. Remember, that metal tube is always measured by its O.D., or outer diameter), you can cut a short length of it and fabricate

one end of it to serve as the antenna mount. This can be as simple as welding a large washer to the end of the tube and opening up the hole to accommodate the antenna. Next to the antenna hole be sure to drill a small 1/4-inch hole to fit a small drain tube into. Otherwise, as I mentioned before, whenever it rains or you wash your car, the tube will fill up with water. So add a drain hole or tube, to which you can attach a length of rubber hose, and remember to route the hose straight down so it does not kink or trap dirt.

Until recently, the only way to create an opening for the antenna tube has been to cut a hole in the fender or panel the size of the tube's O.D., and then cut and trim

The three tubes are tack welded at one place on each tube so they can again be leveled. The depth mark on the tube helps to locate them all at the same depth.

After they are tacked in place, the tubes are checked with a level. They can then be welded permanently in place.

With a Sawzall, remove the top section of the tubes about 1/4 inch above the fender. Don't get too close to the fender or you may cut through. You can grind the tubes flush if you want.

Using an air grinder and an abrasive disk, take the remaining bit of tube down to the fender. If you want to "french" the top of the tubes, leave them at about 1/4 inch and clean up the ends to be molded into the fender.

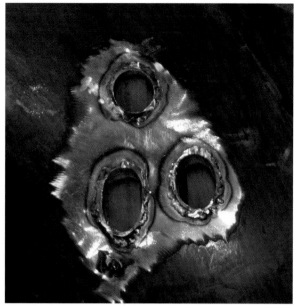

As you grind the metal you may find spots that need to be re-welded. This is the time to do it. This is normal, so don't put the welder away too soon.

A half-round or radiused cheese grater, or Surform file, made by Stanley tools is good for removing the top layer of filler once it becomes "rubbery." If you try this too early you will clog the grater and find they are next to impossible to clean, so wait until the filler is almost set.

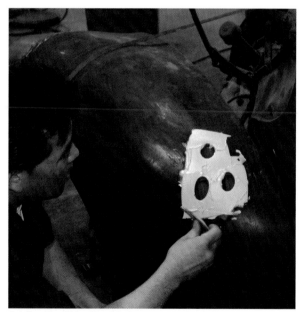

Sanding should begin with about an 80-grit sandpaper and progress down to about 220 grit or finer.

Evercoat also makes a good-quality primer in a "rattle can" that will save you having to clean a gun after just a little body repair. Save the spray gun for the larger jobs.

until the tube can be welded at the desired angle. The way to do this was to hold the tube above the fender or area where you will be sinking the antenna and tilt it or hold it straight up. Then a mark would be traced around the tube for the hole location. This is largely guesswork so you must be careful or you will wind up hacking a large hole in your fender. Another hit-or-miss method of marking the spot is to take the car outside at noon (while the sun is straight overhead) and hold the tube in position and mark around the shadow. This will only work if the sun (or other light source) is directly over the tube.

To make this part of sinking an antenna a more precision

operation, I have designed a tool for this that I call my "laser hole marker." To use this tool, I started by drilling a small pilot hole in the location where I wanted to mount the antenna and then bolt the laser hole marker into the hole. After leveling the fixture with a torpedo level, I turn the laser on and slowly rotate the tool so that the laser creates a track of light on the fender exactly where the opening needs to be cut. If you like to make precision measurements like I do, you can design your own tool for this or buy one like mine to hold a laser pen at the proper distance for duplicating the radius of the tube. By angling the laser mounting rod, an oblong pattern will be shown

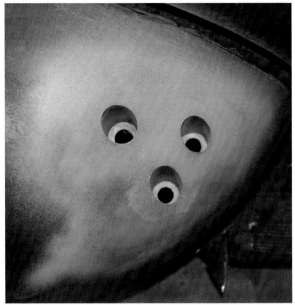

Spray the primer into the holes and to the bottom or rust will come to see you. If the tube is too deep it will be more difficult to get primer and paint into the holes, so keep them fairly shallow—about 4 inches deep is good.

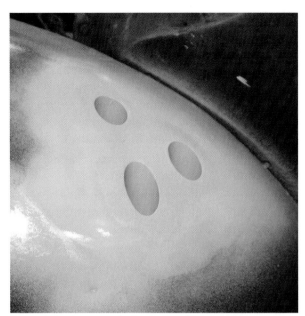

Lay on a liberal amount of primer so you fill the small imperfections and think of primer as a sprayable filler. It is designed to fill small imperfections, but do not let it run.

The base of the electric antenna can then be installed from the bottom of the fender. You may want to take the fender off for this step unless you love laying on your back on cold concrete.

on the car and can be traced for an angled antenna tube.

I always start with a tube length that is longer than needed. As I spot weld it into place I'll have a portion of the tube to hold on to, making it easier to tweak it around into proper alignment as I level it after welding. Once it's tack-welded at the exact angle that I want, I weld it opposite of the first weld and then 90 degrees on each side of the first two welds. This sequence of tack welding will insure that the pull from each weld will not affect the position of the tube. Applying intermittent tack welds also minimizes the chance of warping the panel.

After the entire circumference of the tube is welded,

I found that adding the mounting nut, mounting washer, base and rubber gasket to be a bit difficult to keep in the socket as it is installed. By using tape or clay, the parts can be held together and installed as one piece.

Laying the fender down allowed access to both sides.

A battery charger makes it easy to test the antenna for movement and alignment. Don't forget to add the drain tube and bottom mounting strap.

the installation of the tube is complete, save for cutting it down flush or "frenching" it. If you are going to french the opening, let the excess tube stick up a little higher and then mold it in. If not, cut it flush and grind it down, being careful not to cut through any part of the weld.

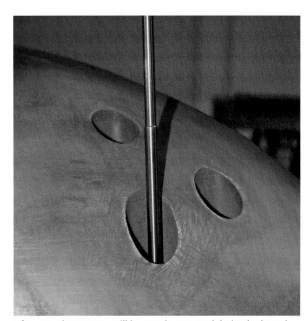

Of course, the antenna will have to be removed during bodywork and painting, but until it is, have fun making it go up and down.

After the top was chopped I decided to radius the rear top of the back door to blend with the overall design, so we ground the area down to allow us to mark the metal before cutting.

The inside of the jamb is also squared off and will need to be radiused. The outside of the jamb will also need to be cut and shaped.

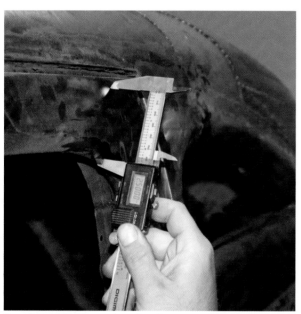

The width of the surround needs to be measured all the way around the window.

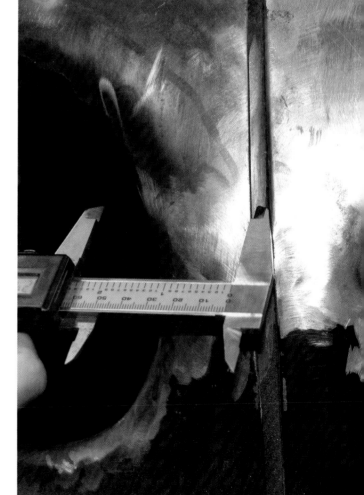

The width of the surround is also not equal on this car, which makes this a tricky job. Many doors can be radiused without cutting the jamb or changing the width of the surround.

Cutting Corners: A Fast and Easy Way to Radius the Doors

Customizing has evolved over the years from radical changes in design to subtle touches that are sometimes barely noticeable. Rounding, or radiusing, the corners of doors, decklids or hoods is a really old trick that looks so clean and unassuming that many people don't even know you have performed the modification, that is unless you've done it incorrectly.

Rounding corners is a simple and fast modification that requires little in the way of experience, but does require a

I use tape for the initial layout of the cut because it can be moved and re-laid without leaving a mark on the body. You simply "play" with the shape until you like the look.

Once you have the tape line the way you like it, you are ready to mark it in ink by simply tracing along the edge of the tape.

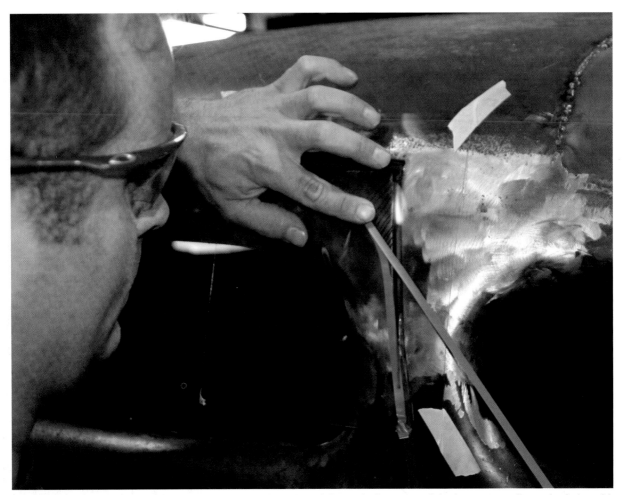

Keeping in mind that we are doing both sides of this car, we lay a piece of clear Makrolon on top of the door corner and trace the design with tape and felt tip marker.

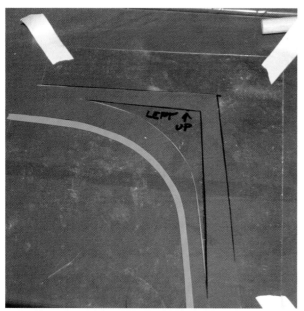

We traced on the plastic so that, by flipping the plastic over after cutting it out, it can serve as the pattern for the opposite side.

With an abrasive cutoff wheel in an air grinder, we are ready to trim the door corner to the tape. We are only roughing with the cutoff wheel.

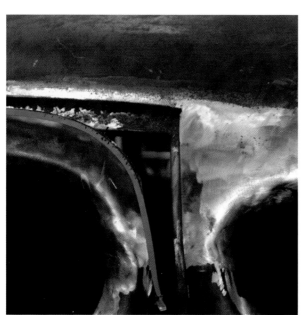

The new corner is beginning to take shape.

shrinker and stretcher, as well as a handful of simple body tools. The best way to start is to figure out what radius you will be using on your doors and the rest is just by the numbers.

To determine the correct radius, you will simply find the radius of the door opening and calculate the increase in radius at the door edge. For instance, if the door jam has a 1-inch radius and the door face extends out an extra inch, the new radius is 2 inches. Mark the radius on the outside of the door and then cut it with a small carbide cutting wheel. After making the cut, grind the edge of the door into a perfect arc. Cutting the corner off of the door will

The door already looks better with the corner cut off, but it will require a bit of work to fill in the corner.

The inner door frame must be trimmed back and re-worked so it nestles into the soon-to-be-remade corner.

With the corner cut out, we are ready to start making a pattern for the replacement metal.

Again, an air cutoff wheel is employed for trimming back the metal.

Using a small piece of clear plastic, we trace the design for transfer to metal.

This piece of metal is then sheered to size and a flange bent at 90 degrees. These will fit both rear doors.

You might as well make both sides at once, and remember to flip the pattern over or you will have two identical pieces instead of two mirrored pieces.

Remember to constantly check for fit, or you will probably turn your new part into a piece of scrap metal.

We use a pneumatic shrinker and stretcher as well as manual ones. The powered unit is for roughing the part to shape. The hand unit is for detail work.

Small hand-powered metal shrinkers and stretchers are available from many sources and work well, but they might produce blisters on your hand after a few hours.

By stretching the metal in the flange you can produce a curve in the larger section of the metal. It won't be a perfect curve, however, so you may need to tap it into a better shape with the use of a "P" dolly of proper radius.

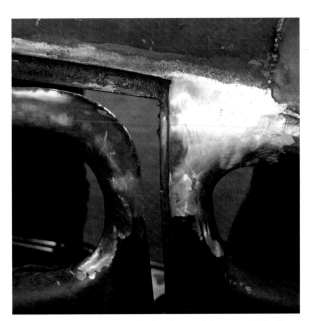
The edge of the door was welded and ground down to the final shape before we started the body jamb radiusing.

To shape the inner body jamb I cut a strip of metal and radiused it over the finished door jam by laying a scuff pad down first. The pad gave me about 1/4-inch spacing between the door and the jamb. This metal will be welded to the body for the start of the inner body jamb.

separate the outer door skin from the door structure, so you will need to weld up the new cut and grind it smooth to finish it off, once again making sure not to grind through the weld.

Now make sure your door is properly aligned to the body before you add the radiused section to the body or you will have a hard time aligning it later. Just as with aligning doors and body panels, do not measure, cut and round corners with the car suspended on jack stands as this will affect how the door hangs in place.

To make a template, place clear plastic in the corner. Try to trim the plastic so it fits perfectly into the corner. Next take a felt tip marker and mark around the radius onto the pattern material. This will be the template for the material that will fill the corner, so set it aside for later use.

Next measure the height of the step and the distance for the radius from start to finish and transfer these measurements to the metal you will use. Next, take a diagonal measurement for the top and bottom step that will reach the corner from midway along the arc.

The piece is welded in the upper rear area of the door jamb and checked for fit by closing the door. You should have the same spacing around the door when it is shut. If you don't, you will need to modify this section, or just move it and re-weld it into place.

Next we fabricated the body door corners that will fill in the gap in the body left over after cutting down the doors. These fillers will be formed in the shape of a flattened "Z." One end of the "Z" is stretched and the other is shrunk, forming a curved shape.

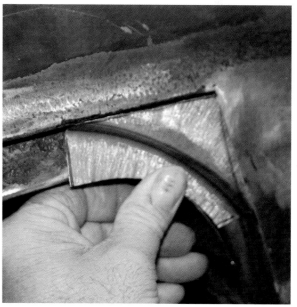

Check the fit as you form the part to make sure you do not over-bend it.

Lay out your pattern on the metal or transfer these numbers to the metal so it can be bent into a "Z" configuration with the height of the step matching the same height of the door jamb. Many door jambs taper as the radius matches the top frame and the rear frame. This taper will have to be matched to fit exactly into the area in which it is intended.

Now stretch one leg of the "Z" using a hand or pneumatic stretcher, then shrink the other leg of the "Z" using a shrinker. Repeat the stretch/shrink process alternately as

you rotate around the new piece of filler metal. Take the template you made earlier and match it to the piece you are making until you are happy with the results of the radius. Be sure to alternate and go slowly as you move from one end of the corner piece to the other. You may need to go back and forth a few times as you get closer to the finished part, but try not to shrink or stretch too much as it will be harder to reverse the process than to simply stretch or shrink a little bit more.

If the part does not match and it looks like a lost cause,

The door jamb is filled in with the fabricated piece of metal and is ready for grinding.

This is one of those small jobs that can make a large difference in the finished product. It does not take a lot of time or cost, and does not even require a lot of skill, but has a very pleasing outcome.

Be sure to weld up all the seams all the way around the newly installed metal, or you will see cracks develop down the line as your car flexes during normal driving.

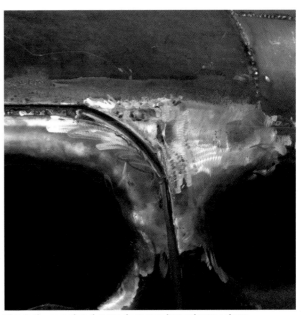

This is the completed outer door area just prior to primer.

scrap it and start over with a new piece of metal. These corners use more of your patience than raw materials, and sometimes it is faster and easier to start fresh after a mistake than it is to continue with a part that has been overworked.

After you get the radius to match the pattern you can start fitting it to the car. This process is as simple as holding it in place and checking for obstructions as you swing the door to a closed position. You may need to fit and trim a few times to get it perfect but it is well worth the time it takes.

Grind the jamb area next and tack weld the new part in place. Once it is set exactly where you want it, finish it off with a good bead and you are ready to grind the metal and mold it. If done correctly the car will look like it came from the factory this way. The last step on the way to painting is to give the newly rounded corner area a coat of good quality primer. Keep in mind the process is the same for radiusing hood and trunks except on these larger panels you will cut the part of the hood or trunk and re-weld it to the body as you make the weatherstrip channel.

This is a shot of the headlights with rings machined to fit the bottom of the lamp, holding them flat on the table.

A More Advanced Project: Frenched Headlights and Taillights

The sign of real customizing is when you get into frenching the headlights and taillights. These projects are not all that hard to do when you consider the rewards. Each headlight will take about a day, as will each taillight, so figure on a couple of weekend's worth of work.

You will start by taking out the old headlights and taillights and putting the parts aside, as some of the parts will be reused on the new design. This will be the hardest part of the project because on "old" cars, the lights are oftentimes rusted in place and the screws are all but impossible to remove by traditional methods. This may mean you'll need to try a chemical approach. For this, a can of WD-40 or Liquid Wrench is just what you need. If you spray it on the bolts or screws and wait a few minutes, most headlamp and taillamp assemblies can be removed fairly easily. If this fails to work you always have the option of an abrasive cut-off tool, or a drill, to drill out the screws.

Frenched Headlights

The headlight bucket is the main part you will be recycling, along with the lamp and many of the mounting

This frenched headlight project will require some type of vacuum-forming machine, unless you can scrounge up a set of headlight assemblies from a wrecking yard. We decided to make our own.

screws. There are a number of ways to do the rest of the job and we will cover a few. In the case of the old '40 Ford, I found that the 65-year-old headlight buckets were too far gone, which was OK since I wanted to design a set of newer and smaller double headlamps instead. So I figured this would take a simple call to the auto parts store for a set

Place the parts on the table, making sure that they have draft, or they will tend to stick in the plastic.

The plastic, once cooled, will be a replica of the part you are using, but it will be a little larger.

Each piece is then trimmed for use.

This part becomes the bucket for the lamp. Unless you can find one, this is the best way to make one.

of bulbs, trim rings, housings and adjuster hardware.

Well, it was not that simple as I found out that the buckets or housings are not sold in auto parts stores and I was told to start going to the wrecking yards for what I wanted. Time is money and I value my time more that wasting a day in a wrecking yard, so I ordered some plastic and started making a "plug" to fabricate my own headlight buckets! This way I could get them exactly the way I wanted them and have the option to make spares if needed.

I first started by making a set of caps to fit over the three electrical prongs on the back of the headlight. This cap would protect the prongs from being damaged during the vacuum forming process. Then I made plastic rings from a large piece of PVC plastic pipe. The rings were for holding the headlight bulb level on the table during the vacuum-forming process. I used the headlamp bulb for part of the plug. I made two of each part so that I could form two headlamp buckets at a time. This would save some plastic as the table that I was using has a 2 x 4-foot platform.

The plugs were placed on the table and set about 1/3 of the way in from the edge and an equal distance apart from each other to minimize the "webbing" effect of the plastic between parts as it forms. Webbing is basically a wrinkle in the plastic that occurs if the parts are tall and too close together. The plastic melts to itself and forms a bridge-like rib in between the parts. Spacing the parts an adequate distance apart will help eliminate this problem. If you get a small web it is not a big deal and in most cases will not weaken the parts, but a big web could separate and weaken the part substantially.

A sheet of 1/8-inch-thick 2-x-4-foot ABS plastic was added to the forming machine and then heated to a soft pliable state, at which point the plastic was pulled down to the plugs. At the flip of a switch, the vacuum is activated allowing the air to be pulled out of the space between the plastic and the platform. This draws the plastic into direct contact with the plug on the platform that we made from the parts. This process replicated the contour and shape of

The front of the '40 has been stripped and is ready for the frenching project.

The headlight mounting base that we made out of aluminum is held up for a quick look to see if it will fit.

To hold the lights at the same angle, we ran a piece of angle aluminum across the face of the base plates and clamped them together.

Next, I got a piece of U-Bend tubing (used for building exhaust) and held it up to see if it would work for a leading edge. I wanted a fat leading edge, not the skinny ones that are more common.

I ripped the tube down the center and made two sections out of one tube — a left and a right.

A test is made to see if it looks OK tilted forward. I liked it.

A bit of a fancy cut is made on another piece of U-Bend. This will be the bottom return into the body. On this U-Bend a slice is made at each end as it is laid flat on the band saw table. We needed four of these parts.

Each of the slices is then held to the bottom of the first U-Bend and marked for length.

These sections are then welded to the bottom of the first piece allowing the curve to turn back into the fender at the bottom.

They can still be tilted up to the proper angle after the tack weld at the bottom. Then a plastic pattern is made and copied in metal.

This piece is added to the top of the fender and tack welded in place.

the part to an exact dimension that would be hard to do by any other method. Once the formed plastic has a chance to cool, it can be lifted and the parts removed. After the buckets were formed and trimmed out to fit the headlights I attached the trim ring and bucket together with the headlight bulb between them and the fit was perfect.

The next part is a bit advanced for a beginner and requires the use of a CNC mill. You might want to locate a machine shop in your area that will accommodate a small custom order. I made my headlight mounting plates from a sheet of 6061-T6 aluminum on a CNC mill. This can be done with a band saw or saber saw and hand tools.

I continued by propping up the headlight mounting plate temporarily so I had something to measure from. This step allows you to calculate where the metal is to be removed from and where the headlights look good. As soon as I had the location for the headlights and the surrounding metal removed from in front of them, I made a set of temporary brackets that could be riveted or tack welded in place

Eddie Paul's Custom Bodywork Handbook

Use the same pattern for both sides. This guarantees that they look the same. Be sure to flip the pattern over for the other side.

The headlight extensions are looking symmetrical from the front and the patterns are fitting up nicely.

Another check of the headlight for fit and we are still looking good. You cannot check things too often. One weld can warp the metal enough to keep a part from fitting.

Here, I am fitting a sheet of plastic to the side of the fender for a pattern. We use clear plastic so you can see where it touches the fender.

during the layout of the surrounding metal work.

The leading edge of the new frenched headlight should be made from either a bar or tube. Most of the time I start with a rod around the new opening and build to it. This rod can be of any size, but what I have found to work the best is a piece of 1/4-inch hot rolled rod. I like hot rolled because it is much easer to shape than cold rolled and with a little heat, or even without heat, it can easily be bent into a smooth curve and added to the fender to check fit and design.

If you think the rod is about the shape you want and you are ready for fine tuning, you can tack weld it at the bottom of the rod to the fender, which will allow you to still tilt and rotate it into proper alignment or even fine tune the opening bend if need be. Once the (1/4-inch rod) outline for the headlamp opening is tacked on and adjusted you may want to cut a short piece of the same rod and fit it to the top of the fender and the top of the newly formed headlight ring. This will hold it in place better and

allow you to make a pattern without knocking it out of alignment. This can become part of the structure if you want or be removed later once the metal is put in place.

At this point we could start on inner fender headlight bucket that we removed from the original fender. Some people remount it in the same opening and just add a frenched extension around it, while others remount the headlamp further forward. This is totally a matter of choice and the ultimate design will dictate what you need to do for your particular application.

Next I laid out some pattern material to trace a pattern to use later as I transfer the design to metal. This pattern should be checked from one side to the other to be sure it is exactly the same or it will be painfully obvious that the car is hand built. Always make one pattern and flip it over for the opposite side. If it does not fit, then find out why before you move on or weld anything in place or you will have to tear it off. It is a common mistake to just want to get on with the project and forget a small measurement

After transferring the pattern to metal it is run through the English wheel to bow the panel out slightly before it is added on to the car.

A few tack welds and the panel is ready for shaping on the car. For this, we use a hammer and dolly.

At this point we moved to the inside of the extensions. This is the area we are going to fill with metal, so once again a pattern is made and transferred to metal.

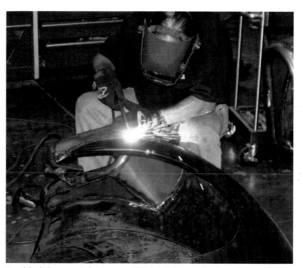

I welded the areas that were a bit hard to reach when the fender was on the car. I took the fender off at this point to do the under-fender cleanup, such as trimming away the extra metal.

error but if left unchecked and unfixed, that tiny error can and will snowball into a larger problem later on.

I chose a slightly different approach to the headlight treatment this time around because "most people" use a 1/4-inch rod for the leading edge, but I like to set trends, not follow them. So to coordinate with the roundness of the '40 I decided to use something a little different—"U-Bend" tubing! U-Bend is a pre-bent tubing that come in a variety of diameters and is available on the Internet with a simple search. This tubing is mandrel-bent into a "U" shape (thus the name) and is intended primarily for exhaust system fabrication. Since the mandrel bends of these pieces are much tighter in radius than what I can make on my shop's hydraulic bender, I keep a supply of U-bends for many things other than just making headers and exhaust pipes.

I decided to use a section of U-Bend tubing for the leading edge of the frenched headlights on my '40 Ford.

By splitting a U-Bend along its length, I could use the two halves for the left and right headlight enclosure. By cutting another U-Bend I made the ends of the lower section where the leading edge rolls into the body. This was tack welded onto the lower section of the fender and the top was pulled out slightly for looks. Once the leading edge was tacked in place, the metal was cut (after the patterns were made) and the custom cut pieces were added, alternating from one headlight to the other so the symmetry from left headlight to right headlight was consistent. For this, the fenders had to be removed and reinstalled a few times just to get to the areas that are hard to reach for welding and shaping.

When the leading edge was tilted forward, I had to remount the fenders on the car, making sure the car was level. I marked a reference line which would later be used for alignment with a laser by setting the fender on the shop floor, leading edge down, and supporting the lower edge up to align the mark on the fender with a 360-degree laser

An inner headlight flange was made to clean up the inside of the fender and make it look solid.

The pattern is transferred to metal and the metal put in a slip roll about midway. A carpenter square is used for alignment.

These are the frenched headlights after all the metal was welded and the only thing left was the bodywork and a paint job. This job took about 8 hours to complete and has changed the looks of the front of the '40 without a lot of cost.

line. This allowed me to ensure that the fender was sitting perpendicular to my reference line and not to the front leading edge of the fender. Then I moved the laser around to shine the line into the headlight bucket area and transferred the laser line to the plastic pattern that I had previously added to the area. This showed me where to cut the pattern so I would have the rear of this pattern match the mark I had made on the fender. With this angle the same I knew that the flat portion of metal I would be adding to the rear of the cutout would be vertical to the ground, even though the leading edge of the headlight was not.

The rear of the '40 is a perfect choice for sunken taillights, as it has a high crown and flows nicely into the body.

Using a 1/4-inch drill bit, we drilled out the rusted bolts from the top side.

The tubes are lined up so they can all be fit into the holes as the holes are cut in the fenders.

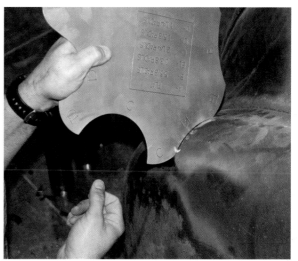

We use a large radius gauge to check the curve of the fender, and then take the gauge to the workbench, saving us multiple trips to the car re-checking the curve.

Frenched Taillights

To complement the custom look of the headlights, the next treatment was to sink the taillights into the rear fenders. Following my propensity for multiples of three, I decided that the rear end of the '40 would have a total of six taillights, three on the left and three on the right. In order to do this we had to start by finding the right taillights. The factory Ford taillights might have been quite stylish back in 1940, but were not the right look for what I had in mind. I wanted a simple, small-diameter round light with bright illumination. For this I contacted Jane Barroga at United Pacific Industries Inc. and she was kind enough to send me six of the 2-inch roadster LED lights in red and two in amber. This would cover not only my taillights, but my front turn signals as well. They are simple to wire and come with a pigtail consisting of two leads that connect to your car's existing harness. However, they do not have any means of mounting except for gluing or double-stick tape.

Since I will never be replacing them as they appear to last forever, I opted to make an adaptor plate that would glue to the taillight but screw to the inside of the taillight tube.

The next job was to figure out where I wanted them to be on the fender. Sunken taillights are not a new fad by any stretch of the imagination. In fact, they are one of the oldest custom treatments around and are still one of the most popular treatments today.

The anatomy of a sunken light is fairly simple and, depending on the size and shape of the taillight, you can use just about anything for this modification. Just as an old shock absorber tube works well for a sunken antenna, a length of exhaust pipe can be used for taillights.

The tube can also be made from a flat piece of metal that is rolled around a pipe or in a sheet metal roller. If you opt for the flat steel sheet rolled into a tube you will need to know how to measure the piece of steel for the rolling of a tube, and this will require a little math. If, for instance,

Eddie Paul's Custom Bodywork Handbook

The base rod of the marking tool is then leveled with a 6-inch bubble level and we are ready to attach the laser head.

The is the prototype of the laser hole marking tool. It works just like the refined version, which has fewer parts.

I drilled a hole large enough to fit the end of my nibbler in and then rough cut a hole for final trimming with a set of aviation snips. You just have to stay inside the lines.

The area around the holes is then ground down for welding.

you want to sink a taillight that is 3 inches round. Simply multiply that diameter of three times pi or (3.1415989) and the result (9.424) will equal the width of the metal needed to roll a 3-inch-diameter tube. If you plan to sink that taillight 4 inches into the fender, add an extra 6 inches (which will be trimmed off after welding) and the final dimension for the sheet of metal to roll is 9.424 x 10 inches. Properly rolled, the tube will have a diameter of 3 inches and a length of 10 inches. This easy formula will apply to calculating sheet metal measurements for any size tube, as long as it's round.

Like the sunken antenna, the end of the tube where the taillight will mount can be capped off with sheet metal or a large washer. To fabricate the cap, you can trace the diameter of the tube onto a piece of metal, cut it out and weld it on. It will be easier to drill all the holes in the plate before you weld it to the tube, but this may vary depending on the taillight you will be using.

Marking the location for the taillight is the most critical part of sinking a taillight, especially if you're planning to install multiple lights on each side. The reason why some sunken taillight installations go awry is because of the method, or lack of, that people use to mark the hole for the tube to fit into. The first step in locating the left and right taillight locations is to find an exact center point at the rear of the car that you can take measurements from. Measure from the center point to the spot on the left fender where you want to install the light. If your center reference point is dead center and both left and right fenders are aligned properly, your taillight location marks will be perfectly even.

Next, drill a small pilot hole exactly on your marks around which you will scribe the circumference of the tube for cutting. Transferring the circumference to the fender is fairly simple if you're lucky enough to be working with a flat surface, but in most cases, that part of the fender will be

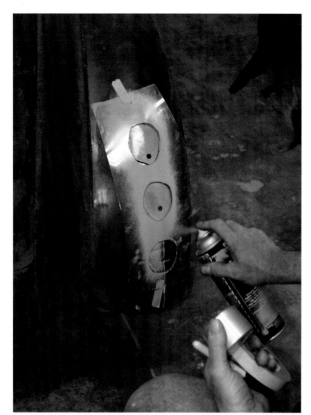

At this point I traced a pattern and transferred it to the other fender.

The passenger's side was nibbled out to match the driver's side.

The tubes slipped in with little effort and were pushed to the proper depth for welding.

The tubes can be adjusted for depth and angle by simply moving them into proper alignment and adding a single tack weld to hold their position.

contoured. To mark the tube circumference onto a curved surface, you will need to devise a tool that will allow you to make one clean cut. Otherwise, it will be a matter of repeated trimming and fitting before you're able to insert the tube properly.

The tool that I came up with is the same one used on the sunken antenna; very similar to a compass. The difference is that my tool can be attached using the 1/8-inch pilot hole, and it is adjustable to compensate for any contour. Making a tool such as this might at first seem to be an

extra step, but it's an extra step that actually saves time and allows you to make a clean, accurate hole for the sunken taillight.

Any good machine shop can turn one of these little tools out in just a few hours, or if you have a lathe in your shop you can do it yourself. I fitted my tool with a pen laser, but you can attach a felt tip marker. Once you have a tool for marking the circumference, you attach it at the pilot hole and rotate it as you extend the marker across the surface of the fender. And you will have marked a hole on a curved

The tubes were aligned with each other and welded in place.

With the aid of a Sawzall, I cut the ends off the tubes about 1/8 inch from the surface of the body.

Switching to sandpaper of about 36 grit, we took the surface down to where we just started seeing metal. At that point, we switched to a finer grit.

The edges were ground down to the surface and we were ready for filler.

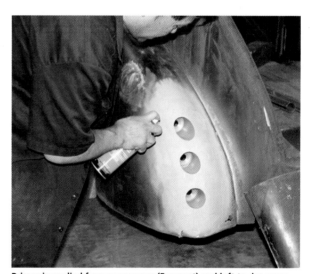

Primer is applied from a spray can (Evercoat) and left to dry as we moved on to another area of the car.

surface. Now you can make your cut with precision. Slip the tube into the hole and adjust it for alignment using a level and a tilt bracket on two sides of the tube. After the tube is welded into place, trim the excess tube off on both sides, leaving a lip extending about 1/4 inch that will serve as the lip for molding into the fender. You can also grind the excess tube off flush, but leaving a lip and molding means it is "frenched."

This same basic procedure can be used to "french" other parts of a vehicle, including sidemarker lights, license plates, antennas, emblems etc.

This pristine 1972 Mustang is about to undergo the knife at our shop. It will be morphed into "Frankenstang."

Fender Flares

I wish I could show you all of the sets of fender flares we have fabricated out of steel over the years! When flares were gaining popularity back in the early 1970s, most custom shops were working with fiberglass. My shop, Customs By Eddie Paul, was one of the first to use steel for every fabrication job, and that included fender flares,

The main reason for flaring a fender is to increase the clearance when larger tires and/or offset wheels are used. A flare can be anything from a mild extension of the fender lip to a totally redesigned fender and anything in between. Flares can be fabricated in a number of ways, but having built so many of them over the years, I've pretty much settled on my own way of doing them.

As in most customizing jobs, it helps to have a design in mind before you start. The easiest type of flare to fabricate can be made by cutting along the wheel opening and pulling the existing lip out just enough to clear the tires. The open space between the fender and the lip is then filled with sheet metal. If you have a more elaborate style in mind, or if you have very wide tires to make clearance for, you will most likely have to cut a large portion of the fender away and fabricate the entire flare.

We started the Mustang flare project by putting in a Currie rear end with disk brakes and bought a set of tires for the rear—not just any tires. I went with the MT tires, the wide ones.

This is a few days into the flare, and at this stage I am only interested in getting tire clearance by cutting out the wheel well inner area. The round bar is for a reference of the opening.

Each section and about 12 to 18 inches long and about 4 inches wide. A 1-inch flange is then bent along one side. This flange is then put in a stretcher, and stretched to make the piece arc to match the opening.

The inner well is welded into place as it is made and bent to fit.

Adding one piece at a time allows for adjustments as you move along the radius.

The accompanying photos in this section illustrate the fabrication of a not-so-typical and very large set of flares on a '72 Mustang fastback. Mustangs of all years have an inherent problem with tire clearance whenever a larger wheel-and-tire combination is added. The wheels and tires on the rear of this Mustang are the largest street-legal size available, so we definitely had a clearance issue. The problem was solved with an equally massive set of flares that were fabricated in a short span of two days, albeit by an experienced fabricator. If this is your first attempt at flaring a fender, it will probably take several days per flare to get them right.

Depending on the type of car that you have and the size of the flare that you have in mind, there are a few potential obstacles to be aware of. A large flare can extend beyond the fender area into the rocker panel, bumper, a gas filler door or a side marker light. If this is the case, then the shape of the flare must incorporate these non–fender items in the

Each section of the buck is removable. This allows us to custom cut each one to get exactly what we want.

This project definitely changed and evolved from the original plan. You never know where a customizing project will lead.

This is the rear flare from the rear before the bumper extensions have been added.

From the side, the flares change the whole look of the Mustang.

design, or you'll have to style the flare to avoid overlapping these items entirely.

The first step in fabricating a fender flare at my shop is to create a framework that will provide sufficient clearance around the tires in all positions. The main element of this framework is the wheel opening for which we use 1/4-inch round steel bar that we shape around the tire for a matching contour. The bar is tack-welded at the front and rear points where it connects to the fender. From there I tilted it out to the width that I wanted then checked for clearance with the tire by adding weight to the car (we have several lead-shot bags that we use for simulating a load on the suspension) and bouncing it. Once I was convinced that we were not going to grind the tires to the rims, I continued by adding the inner panels where we had to remove metal from the inner wheel well. This could be riveted in or welded in depending on the fire hazards at hand. Once the inner panels are in and sealed with undercoating, you can start on the outer flare and, depending on the complexity of the shape, you

should be able to knock them out in about a couple days per flare for just the metal work. As a hobbyist working on your own car, don't feel pressured to rush the job to meet a time schedule. Go slow and enjoy the process.

To help maintain symmetry as you build flares, it's best to fabricate the same piece for both left and right flare at the same time. You should remove the wheel and tire so it does not get damaged during welding, but keep it nearby so you can from time to time put it back on to check for clearance. Another caution concerning welding (aside from the obvious fire precautions) is to protect your windows from welding splatter and sparks. Those tiny little beads of hot molten metal will burn and stick to glass on contact. We tape window glass with duct tape whenever any welding takes place.

With the wheel opening bar welded into place, it's time to start adding the sheet metal for the flare. The best place to start is at the top, or center, and work your way down on each side of the flare. Making paper patterns of each

Bucks work great for wheel flare projects. You won't need them after you gain experience, but they are great for learning.

Brian has been building flares for a very long time, so it was hard to get him to go back to using a buck, but this is to show you how it should be done. Here, he is putting a pattern on a plastic sheet so it can be transferred to metal for a section of the flare.

The buck is removable and can be taken off the car at any point and moved to a table for making intricate patterns.

The buck is back on the car and a first "gore" of metal in place. Start from the center and work both ways outward.

section will help you to cut the metal into shape, but plan on doing a fair amount of trimming to fit as you go. Theoretically, each pattern that you make for a flare on one side, should work on the opposite side by simply flipping it over. It doesn't have to be a precise fit here (up to 1/4 inch off is still in the ballpark), but if a pattern doesn't come close to fitting on the other side (remember to flip it over), you'll have to stop and figure out the problem. Assuming that both left and right fenders are straight, it will most likely be caused by a wheel opening bar that has a slightly different arch bent into it, or the distance from fender to bar is different. You must fix this before proceeding.

Once you're back on track, you can continue with the sheet metal patterns and cutting. If your wheel opening bars are perfectly identical from left to right, take your time with the first piece of sheet metal as this is the most critical for left-to-right symmetry. Fabricate both the left and right center pieces of the flare and tack them into place. Then step to the front of the car dead center (or rear of the car

Another gore was in place as Brian trimmed the top area where the metal meets the body. The tool is an extended right angle abrasive cutter from The Eastwood Company.

Customizing Techniques—A New Look at Traditional Custom Bodywork

The gores are tack welded at each corner so you can take them off for trimming. They will be welded up after they are all in place, so we sometimes remove them, trim them and reinstall them.

for the rear flares) and take a visual of both flares at the same time to make sure they are perfectly even. This takes a keen eye and a lot of walking around the car with a tape measure, but this step is the most critical!

My flare fabricator, Brian, has built so many sets of flares that he can spot a slight unevenness at a glance, but he still takes the time with this step of the flares to avoid having to redo them later. He'll tell you that symmetry is all important in flare fabrication. Take every measurement possible to use as a reference, and each one must match from left to right.

Once you have the left and right center pieces tacked into place and everything measures out and looks even, the remainder of the fabrication process is all downhill.

Welding the flares requires a bit of skill and a few tricks to keep everything smooth without warping the metal from the heat build-up. We used to use a product called Moistbestos, which was a concoction of asbestos and something that made a clay-like paste that drew heat away from a panel like nothing I have ever seen before. We now use a similar product. Building a ridge of this stuff along both sides of the weld area before welding will reduce

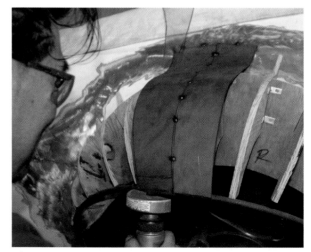

After trimming and tack welding the first gore back on, we started tapping it in near the top for more contour. At this point it looks as if it will no longer be taken off, so we trimmed the bottom to fit.

buckling by a factor of 5 to 1, so it's well worth the effort. Even though you are using a heat reducer, you should still intermittently spot weld the flares by jumping from

Keep moving around the flare from center out, making patterns and pieces as you go. This side took a good long day to fabricate.

Each of the seams is welded as soon as you know you will not be changing them. You can shape each panel before adding it to the flare, or shape it after it is welded onto the car, where it is easier to handle.

This flare is a bit on the radical side, but it shows a worst-case situation of what you could run into. I made the flare run into the door scoop just for kicks.

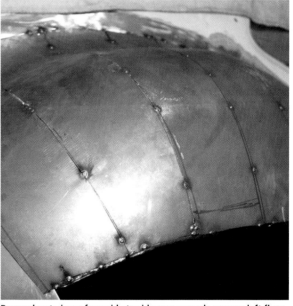

Remember to jump from side to side as you work, or your left flare will probably not look like your right one.

one area to another as far away from the first as you can, then jump to the other side of the car and keep jumping back and forth. This approach will keep the panels from overheating and warping.

As soon as you have welded the entire flares in place it is time to grind the welds down to a smooth flat finish. This is where "weld penetration" becomes important. If the panels you just welded start falling off while grinding, your welds are not deep enough and you will need to run a hotter weld. If, on the other hand, the parts stay in place and the seams look solid, you can add "welder" to your resumé. Once the flares are ground down flat and the flares look

like they are smooth and flat, you can start adding the body filler and start grinding and sanding it to a smooth finish. We use cheese graters and shape the flare to the desired shape before we move on to progressively finer sandpapers, starting with 36 grit down to 180 grit. You can then prime it and start working the surface smoother with paper from 220 down to 360 or 400.

This Mustang has about the biggest set of flares you can build and they are an example of one of the most challenging bodywork projects you can tackle on your car. Milder flares will be much easier.

This is the 1972 Mustang with a modified hood and matching tube-style grille and bumper. The bumper and tubes were fabricated from .125-inch-wall-thickness roll bar tubing for strength.

To start a roll bar bumper you will need to have a way to bend the tubing. Bending a tube on each end will make it look much better. We use a hydraulic mandrel bender for this and started with 2-inch tubing with about 1/8-inch wall.

The steel miter saw is at the proper angle and checked before each cut, just in case it gets knocked out of alignment.

Next, the parts are laid on the ground for double-checking the cut angle. To make it more difficult on myself, I chose to use three different size tubes: the top being 2 inches, the middle 1 3/4 inches, and the bottom 1 1/2 inches.

Rollbar Bumpers

I thought that a set (three to be exact) of roll bar bumpers would look good on my '72 Mustang, but just a set of bent bars would not quite do the trick. I wanted them to look like a custom bumper, not roll bars. The problem was that there was not much you can do with a roll bar tube but bend it, so I decided that to give a slightly different look: I would cut the front ones down the center at an angle and re-weld them back together giving them a slight angle in the center instead of just a radiused bend. This way I could get by bending the outside ends around the fenders and have them disappear into the body, into holes just big enough to accept them.

After each tube was checked and cut to length, a piece of round bar was drilled and threaded to accept a bolt. This will be the bumper end mounting system.

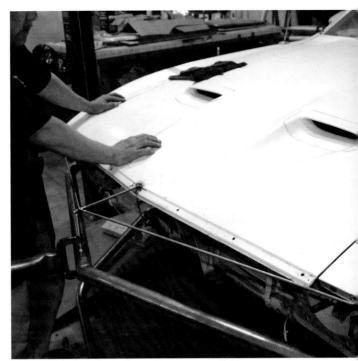

We made a special rig to hold the bumper tubes in place as we fit them to the car. This rig can eliminate the need for a helper.

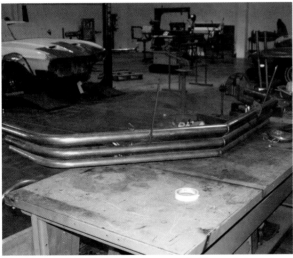

The three tubes are about ready to test again. The next step is to make the mounting brackets and attach them to the car.

You can see the mounting brackets that we made for the front bumpers. Each bumper tube has a bracket welded to it so the bumpers can be separated for chroming.

I would then make the top bumper the largest at a 2-inch outside diameter, the next one down would be 1 3/4-inch outside diameter, and the lowest one would be 1 1/2-inch outside diameter. Each of them would have about 3/4-inch space between them. The mounting brackets were designed to allow each smaller bumper to be set back about an inch from the next higher one. Also, each end would be shorter than the bumper above it, so the overall look was a tapering in toward the lower bumper. By making the bumpers smaller and tapering inward, the look was slightly exaggerated and gave a nice tapered feel to the front end.

This may sound a bit complicated, but it was probably easier to build than it is to explain. It did require a mandrel tubing bender, which could be rented or purchased at a fairly reasonable price. But there is a very bright side to the purchase of a bender: if you ever build a roll cage for yourself or someone else the machine will pay for itself in one job. Many cages cost as much as the price of a bender. When I was building cages for stuntmen in my driveway at home, I could bang out one a day at a cost of about $2,000 a cage. That was then; now they cost much more. I must have built well into the hundreds of cages with that one

Small brackets were made that would later be welded to the bumper tubes so they could be bolted to the mounting bracket that was attached to the car.

The ends of the rear bumpers were cut to the same length and plugged with a threaded bar, as were the fronts. A mounting system was designed to hold the ends of the tube in alignment.

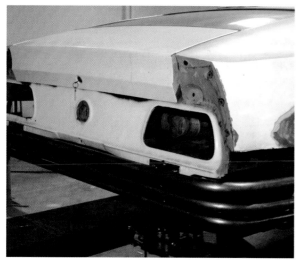

The rear of the 'Stang was starting to look good—boring, but good.

I had to modify the body where it went behind the bumper. Using a piece of welding rod, I bent the approximate shape I wanted to form from sheet metal.

The rear bumper ends are simple wraparounds, but disappear into the body. The body took some modification to allow the bumpers to fit closely.

bender, so the cost was nothing compared to the profit that tool brought in.

As a general rule, most tools will pay for themselves within one or two jobs. So if you do your own work the money you would have to pay someone else to do your job is usually less that what the tools will cost you.

The three bars were added to the bumper bracket we designed to hold the three bars at the proper angle by a small spot weld. This held them in place for alignment and so we could take the whole assembly off and make brackets that would allow the bumpers to be bolted to the bracket. Keep the welds to a minimum, as they need to be

Eddie Paul's Custom Bodywork Handbook

The two sides have to match. We use a tool that contours to the shape of the car, or bumpers, so we can check one side with the other.

The bent panels are run through an English wheel a few times to add a bit of bow to them.

Using a sheet metal brake and a piece of tubing that was split full length, we bent the shape for the side under-bumper body piece. This will be added to the car so it will look as if the bumpers are stock and the body designed to accept them.

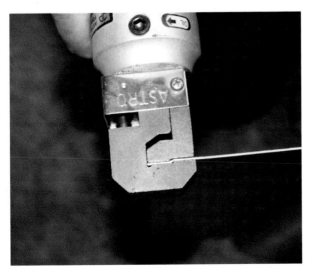

This pneumatic flanging tool will offset the metal to the thickness of the sheet it will be attached to, making the top surface flush after welding.

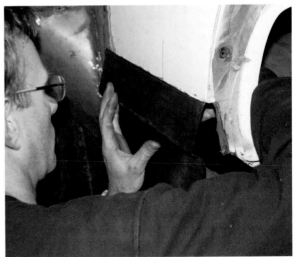

A little trimming and adjusting and it is about ready to weld in place.

I can't help myself! I had to change the rear end while I was adding the rear bumpers. Sometimes, one idea just leads to another.

Getting back to the front bumpers also required that I start a roll pan.

The cover over the front of the left rear bumper ends shows the idea I had to make the bumper disappear into the body.

These mounting tabs were added to the roll bar bumpers so they could be attached to the bumper mounting bracket.

The body is then welded around the area that was just fabricated. Now the car can be sent to the body shop.

brought down flush before the bumpers can be chromed. We marked and cut the ends of the bumpers to the same length. The whole process requireed the mounting and dismounting of the bumpers and brackets a few times, but there was no other way to be sure. We cut out small and welded and welded them into the end of the bumpers. This was also the a method of mounting. Each disc was center drilled and tapped to accept a 1/4-20 thread pitch. These were then inserted in the end of the tubes and welded into place. This way each tube was mounted at each end and at each of the two bumper brackets, or four points. The brackets were designed to mount to the stock bumper mounts and were fabricated from 1/4 x 2-inch cold rolled steel strap.

I had to tell Brian he had a call from a girl just to get him out of the car.

Chopping the Top

Chopping a top is the pinnacle of customizing. Successful top chopping is a combination of planning, design, accurate measuring, precision cutting and good welding followed by meticulous finishing. It can make or break your custom car; too much chop, and the car will look comical, too little and you have basically wasted your time. I once new a guy that chopped his top 1/2 inch! He had to tell me he did it because it was too little to notice. He then went on to answer my unasked question of "Why only a half an inch?" with, "…well it was my first chop and I did not want to ruin the car." He spent as much time removing that 1/2 inch as he would have if he took out 6 inches.

If you are going to chop a top, *chop it!* Don't be afraid.

Restore Or Restyle?

The debate over the merits of customizing verses restoration will probably never be settled. If you restore a car and later sell it, you will find you will get "X" dollars for it based largely on the current market for that car and what other cars like it have sold for. A buyer can simply look up the car's value in the *Collector Car Price Guide* or *Kelly Blue Book* or at a list of auction results and tell you that your car is worth only so much, and he can simply find another one if you don't agree. But if your car is a custom and you want to sell it, you can ask what you want for it (within reason) and nobody can negotiate you down based on the value of any other car.

Some of the cars I have built have gotten more than 10 times what they would have pulled in if I had just restored them. Another point is that I am not getting fleeced each time I need a part. For example, the '40 Ford had no grille and it would set me back a small fortune if I had to find one that was "perfectly stock and original." But the fact

The "B" pillar will be cut out for a chop we intended to be a whopping 6 inches.

The "C" pillar was next to receive the mark showing the section to be cut out.

The famous 1940 Ford rear window was marked for the chopping block. I decided to just cut it out completely and use it for something else in the future.

Using silver duct tape allowed us to make notes on the tape.

The first cut was made with a Sawzall across the top just ahead of the "B" pillar.

that I was customizing the car allowed me to build a "one-off" custom grille out of better material than the factory would have and have a hand-made original grille of my own design. I am a customizer, not a restorer.

I used to restore cars for a company and spent more time trying to find a mirror or a piece of chrome than working on cars. I have a 1952 Rolls Royce Silver Dawn that is totally stock and I will never customize it, as it has too much value as an original and complete car. If I did not have all the parts and if it was not as sound as it is, then it would be a good candidate for a custom. So the rules are not cast in stone, but based on common sense. Now that I think about it, I could just add a bigger engine and do a bit of styling to the front fenders and, what the heck, the top does look a little high…

A rare or limited edition car should probably be left stock. But I have customized rare cars just because I wanted to, and I am sure I have offended someone somewhere. To them, I say: "This is my car and I can do what I want to it.

Eddie Paul's Custom Bodywork Handbook

When all the cuts on the front section of the top were made, the front section was lifted off for cleanup.

The remaining piece of the "A" pillar was trimmed for a better fit. The top will be replaced later.

The top is then laid in place and checked for a general fit. Even with a 6-inch chop, the pillars were almost perfectly aligned.

The Digital Chop!

The most important part of chopping a top is the layout. A new way to calculate your top chop is to first photograph the intended car from the side with a digital camera, making sure that your zoom ratio is set for a normal eye perspective. In 35mm photography, this would be equivalent to a focal length of 50mm (the standard lens that most 35mm cameras come with). Zooming out to a wide-angle view or zooming in to tele-photo close-up will create a distorted perspective of the car. Check your camera lens manual for the correct zoom ratio for normal perspective viewing.

Position yourself on either side of the car at mid-level and mid-car (dead center of the car). If you can, put a piece of cardboard measuring one foot square in the photo for a reference of the size. If you really want to get tricky you can grid the cardboard with a felt tip marker with 1-inch grids. This will give you a way to compare this "scale" to the car. Now take the photo and dump it into a program like Photoshop and cut the top off the car by removing a 6-inch strip from the mid line of the windshield post. This may take a few tries but that is the beauty of doing it on a computer, you can redo it without

I laid out the Photoshop photos for a reference as I worked on the top chop just to see how accurate it would be to use this as a tool for chopping a top.

cutting the car. Then when you have removed the amount you think is right you can lower the roof section in place and see what the car will look like after the chop is complete. Of course, only one of the pillars will line up, depending on where you place the top, but this will still be good enough for a preview. Now it's time to perform surgery on the roof section to get all of the pillar ends to line up with the car body.

Rich moves on to the "B" pillar and the process is repeated as he cut between the lines to remove the offending 6 inches that Ford put in at the factory.

If I ever sell it, I am sure someone will appreciate it enough to buy it." As a customizer, I am not at all concerned about preserving one mark or another. I want a car that reflects my personal design and workmanship.

I have found that the custom route is the way to go, for me anyway, on any rusty or damaged car, as you can easily spend as much on small hard-to-get parts as you did on the complete car when you bought it. So if a car is beyond repair, look at it this way: it will rust away in a scrap yard or could become a show-stopping custom just by removing the rusted body panels and fabricating your own panels with a bit of styling added in. The car will be a great looking and you will be well respected, providing that you do a good job, of course.

The section is gently lifted off and laid on the floor for trimming.

The top is lined up and, four hours after the first lug nut was removed at the beginning of the project, the first welds are applied to the "A" pillars.

Measuring Up

Everybody's heard this before, but it's well worth repeating before you put the saw to metal: "measure twice, cut once." Live by this when you fabricate. If you don't, you can add days of recutting and patching to your chop as you fill in the gaps left over from a poorly measured cut.

Start a top chop by leveling the car where it sits so you have a standard or datum point to measure by. The floor of your garage will be the common point of reference that you know is level to the car (even though the floor itself may not be level). The floor itself does not have to be level, but it does have to be flat. If the floor of the area where you'll be working is too uneven to level the car with, take the time to build some type of framework around the car that you can use to take accurate and consistent measurements from.

I removed the tires and wheels from my '40 Ford and lowered it all the way down onto the ground so that the front axle and rear drums rested on the floor. Then, with the aid of a 360-degree self-leveling laser, I used hardwood blocks to fine tune the level of the car. This way I could always find the level as the laser is moved from side to side. The car was first leveled front to rear and then side-to-side and then again, front to rear. The reason for returning to the front-to-rear leveling is that the side-to-side will affect the front to rear and the front to rear will affect the side to side so you may have to go back and forth a few times. This is a tedious process, but it will help the accuracy of the chop.

Rather than making reference marks with a felt tip marker, I prefer masking tape for one good reason: When (not "if") you must correct a mark because of a change in measurement you can just zip if off, move it and re-tape it down. One drawback to using tape is that you have to remember which edge of the tape to cut on. I say ALWAYS use the outside of the tape so you will not have to remember. And for added insurance, you can mark what edge to cut directly on the tape.

Traditionally, the cutting points of a top chop are

Top Chopping Terminology

A-PILLAR: The front most pillar that is around the windshield

B-PILLAR: The pillar that is second from the front of the windshield

C-PILLAR: The third from the front pillar sometimes called the rear roof pillar.

D-PILLAR: Some four-door sedans or station wagons will have a fourth pillar

The 25 percent rule: There is an old styling rule that pertains to some cars that says that if the glass is 25 percent of the area of the car's body as viewed for the side you have the correct proportions. In many cases this is true. However, I like to take a side shot of the car and either in Photoshop or even with an Exacto blade on a printed photo of the car, cut the section out of the top and see how it looks. This way you can adjust the amount to be cut out before you cut too much. It is better to cut too little than too much.

SQUARE-TOP CARS: Pre-1930 cars that have straight pillars or non-sloping pillars such as the Ford Model A or T these are the easiest cars to chop. The pillars do not slope and you can simply cut out the required section, drop the top down and weld it back on. This kind of job can very easily be accomplished in one weekend.

TURRET-TOP CARS: Cars from the mid-1930's to about 1955 have a rounded top with sloping and

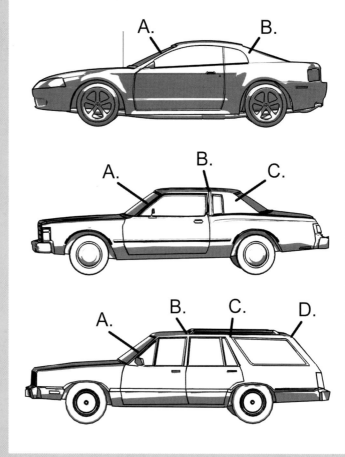

Pillar indentification.

sometimes tapered pillars, bringing the top to a smaller dimension than the base of the pillars. If you chop a section out of the pillars, the top will have to have a strip of metal added to widen it or lengthen it. This is a more difficult chop than the square top.

---

determined using a tape measure and the good old eyeball method. For a two-pillar straight-across chop, this is acceptable (albeit barely). Customizers are a stubborn breed. In spite of the wealth of high-tech tools and devices that are geared for precision work, the tape-and-eyeball method is still in vogue. Well, even for an old school modification on an even older car, I prefer doing it the modern way.

As the price of laser measuring tools has come down to the point of affordability, average guys like us can now make use of this technology to customize our cars. Plus, lasers are just fun to use! Projecting a line with a self-leveling laser makes it much, much easier to mark a horizontal line for the top chop. But once again, this requires that the car is perfectly level before you turn on the laser.

Sizing up the '40 Ford

The steps that I've taken to chop the top of my '40 Ford four-door sedan will be outlined in the following pages. The '40 four-door posed a difficult challenge due to its four-pillar body style. The initial cut to remove the roof section took place over a time span of eight hours. Five of those eight hours were spent leveling, measuring and marking the cut.

The laser was first used to level the '40 by placing it on a tripod (or stand) at approximately the same spot where the digital photo was taken. When you do this, be sure to mark the location of the laser on the floor in case it gets bumped or moved accidentally. Choose a horizontal line on the car such as the bottom edge of the windows to line up the laser

When a top is chopped, I have found it best to leave the doors on the car and clamped shut for a better cut and alignment.

The second section is lowered into place.

Referring to the Photoshop photos, we found the gap to be 1 inch, exactly as predicted.

A temporary piece of bar was clamped in place to hold the second section of the top to the first section.

with. If the red laser line follows the car's horizontal line on both sides, then your car is level. The position of the laser is where you will also use it to locate the cut points for the chop.

Before you start to mark the top for the chop, you must know your angles! Rarely does a top chop involve a straight-across cut with 90-degree vertical pillars. Say you plan to remove a 6-inch section for your chop. The amount removed from a 90-degree vertical pillar would be exactly 6 inches. However, if a pillar is slanted, as most are, the vertical measurement is still 6 inches, but the actual section of the slanted pillar will measure more than 6 inches. Remember, the section to be removed should always be measured 90 degrees vertically to the reference line. Do not measure along a slanted pillar. The reason you need to familiarize yourself with angles is because all tops are different and very few have pillars that will be 90 degrees vertical to the roofline. I highly recommend that you perform a "digital

chop" before actually trying to do the work on a car. Also, locating the cut line with a laser is an almost foolproof way to avoid the confusion with angles.

Marking or taping a continuous cut line around the car for the chop requires projecting a laser line on the side of the car from three positions: the driver's side (left), passenger's side (right), and rear. As you can see in the photos, there will be a small portion on both rear pillars of the car where the laser will not project around. For these spots, you will have to pull the tape or marker line around to join the side cut lines with the rear. Doing this is very similar to taping graphics that would wrap around the car.

Chopping the top requires two separate cut lines, an upper and a lower, be marked or taped off. The distance between the two lines will be determined by the amount of chop that you're planning on. In the case of the '40 Ford, the distance between the two lines was 6 inches all the way around.

This was replaced with a short section of 1/4-inch round bar. All the gaps were coming out as we predicted and this was starting to worry me. How could it be so perfect and why doesn't everybody do this?

The "D" pillar gets cut after the "C" and "B" pillar cuts are finished.

We put the inside window frames aside. We would later cut them down to fit the windows.

Brian cut the rear of the top off. The 6-inch piece is left on the car after the top is removed because it is much easier to let the body hold it in place as you cut it off. If it were left on the top section you would have a heck of a time holding the top as you cut the 6 inches off of it.

With the top removed, you can see the section that needs to be removed from the body.

With all of the glass, trim and interior parts removed, a reciprocating saw with a good metal-cutting blade was used to start our chop. We cut along the top cut line first, keeping the saw blade as straight as possible along the edge of tape until the entire roof section was cut free of the car. This is best done with two people because parts of the roof section have to be manipulated to allow free travel of the saw blade. Also, once the roof section is free, at least two people are needed to lift it from the car.

Once the roof section has been cut all around, the 6-inch section of the chop came next. It is much easier to make the cut around the second, lower cut line with the roof section removed. Be sure to keep the blade angle along the second cut line identical to the first. This makes things line up a lot better when the time comes to graft the roof section back on.

After both cuts were made and the chop section removed all around, we took the entire roof and placed it back onto the car to give us an idea of how much the

The top section was aligned with the back and set in place. It looked like a fit! Even the side windows formed a nice teardrop shape.

roof would have to be sectioned to get each pillar post to line up for attachment. The digital chop that we made on the computer showed exactly where the roof panel would have to be modified within a mere 1/8 of an inch. To get a visual idea, we moved the top forward to line up the A-pillars, then to the back to line up the rear pillars, and then centered it to line up the center pillars.

You have a lot of control over the finished look of the chop as far as how much and where it will wind up. For instance, do you want to center the top and bring the A-pillar back to meet the top or do you want to move the top forward to meet the A-pillar? And then slant the B and C pillar to meet the new location of the top.

If the top is a turret top (slanting inwards from the base of the windows), then you have a lot of choices to make. Something we have once done but not seen anyone else do is to narrow the car to meet the top. It is common to add a strip to the center of the top to bring the top out to meet the new width of the cut down pillars, but to narrow the car to allow the top to remain the unmodified? This is definitely unusual. You can do anything you want if it is your car and your chop, so use your imagination and go wild. You could even shorten the car instead of lengthening the top to fit the bottom posts, but the doors would be shorter by a few inches.

Tackling the tapered chop

Tapered chops are definitely more difficult than a straight chop. They require measuring the top and taping a line that decreases in distance as it progresses forward toward the windshield. This makes angle cuts very complicated, so extra care must be taken in both measuring and cutting. Top chops vary from one car to another, so it's doubtful that you'll be able to find step-by-step instructions to help you with a particular make of vehicle. There have been a

We took the trunk off for access to the top. It will be welded up later, after the top is finished.

With the top tack welded to a rod to hold it in alignment, we can start making a piece of metal to fill in the gap.

A plastic pattern is made and the part duplicated in steel and run through the English wheel a few times for some shape.

I then cut a strip to fill in the gap across the top and bent it to shape. I also put a flange along each edge.

lot of tech-type articles written on the subject, however, so it might help to do a little Internet searching on chopping a top. I found a few postings that might cover some of the variables that you'll encounter, plus a lot of photos that show other vehicles being chopped. If you're lucky, you might even find something published showing how a chop was performed on your model vehicle.

The first step to chop my '40 Ford was the removal of everything that can burn—people, animals, seats, door panels and headliners. When you remove your headliner, pay close attention to the headliner top bows. They are almost priceless when you need them, so take care of them and mark them as to which part of the top they came from.

Take a marker or use the tape and mark each pillar for cutting, and also run a strip of tape across the top at each location to be cut. The tape will provide a precise line to follow that will help you maintain a reasonably straight line as you cut. I cut across the top first to lighten the top, whereas many people just cut the top off in one piece and

have to have help moving it around and trying to locate it. If it was first cut across the top into sections, each section will weigh much less and can easily be maneuvered into position. Then remove the horizontal sections of the pillars. If you do what we did, lower the front section first into position and tack weld the pillars. Then step back and do a sanity check. It's too late to turn back at this point, but you might want to do look things over one final time before you start welding for real.

To hold the rear section of the top you can make temporary blocks out of wood or metal that will hold the back of the front section of the top up to the correct height as you weld the front pillars in place. Then move back one section and do the same to the roof, removing the pillar sections and lowering that section of the top, then the next section until you have lowered the complete top one section at a time. As the sections are lowered you may find the cuts are not exactly straight and there are gaps between the two sections. You can make strips of metal to fill these

Eddie Paul's Custom Bodywork Handbook

The filler plate was added to the front gap.

The rear top section was cut lengthwise and overlapped to bring down the bow that we had in the rear widow area. This was held with a clamp so it could be changed if necessary.

The rear window area was also trimmed a bit to meet the upper trunk line.

The top insert panel is fastened in with a set of Clecos by first drilling a 1/8-inch hole and then adding the Clecos as we moved across the top.

areas. What we do is shear a few strips at different widths just to have on hand so when (not if) this happens, you will have them handy. We have also cut some 1/4 inch round rods to tack weld along the drip rail to temporarily hold the top in alignment as we move along. I also made some pieces to fill the gaps in the roof where it was cut and moved to align with the pillars. The sections were measured by laying down masking tape next to the cut, then marking the tape at both ends where the metal was to be cut. Then the tape was transferred to a sheet of metal and the marks transferred to the metal. I have found masking tape will not stretch and works better than a tape measure to contour across the roof and then be transferred to the metal. The rear triangular roof sections were traced to a piece of clear Vivak with a felt tip marker and then cut out with scissors. The Vivak was then laid on top of a piece of metal and the metal cut out and checked for fit. At this point, if no other trimming is required, the pieces can then be inserted and welded in place.

Glass-cutting equipment:

1. white grease pencil
2. safety glasses
3. gloves
4. 3/4-inch and 2-inch masking tape
5. tape measure
6. glass cutter
7. denatured alcohol
8. single-edge razor blades
9. sand blaster
10. piece of rubber strip the length of the windshield approx. 24 inches wide
11. heavy cardboard
12. glass grinder
13. windshield support/stand
14. propane torch/butane lighter
15. satin finish black aerosol paint

It takes two people to do this part of the job. I held the insert plate up with a piece of wood as Brian tack welded the panel in place. We always start from the center and work both ways toward the outside, alternating from one side to the other.

With the filler strip about 80 percent in place, we can see how the top is starting to get that good old factory curve. At this point we are about 8 hours into the chop.

Tips:

- Automotive safety glass has a thin plastic laminated between layers of glass.
- Curved glass is normally safety glass.
- Tempered glass cannot be cut.
- An alternative to glass is polycarbonate plastic. Check your local laws concerning the use of non-DOT glass.

Doors and Glass

The door frames are the next job at hand, and you should take each of them one at a time. I start at the front and move rearward. You should also work form the front drivers side to the front passenger side then the rear drivers side to the rear passenger's side. Never do all the windows on one side of the car and then proceed to the other side. This will make it much harder to keep the windows the

For the top of the "A" pillar to align with the bottom of the "A" pillar we had to make a diagonal cut and spread the post into alignment. You can see the ground weld above the cut weld.

At this point we went back to working on the rear top insert. We jump around welding different parts so the heat in any one area is kept to a minimum.

The back window upper frame is welded at the rear.

This form of tack welding is the best way we found to keep the heat on the metal down. We go back and weld between each spot until we are totally welded up.

same from right to left. The door frames will not match exactly, so be prepared to do some fancy metal fabrication to fill in the curves around the front and rear sections.

Next comes the original glass, which will also have to be removed and stored for cutting down or for patterns. Once again, mark the location of the pieces. This will save you time on the reinstall or for the new patterns. Once the top is chopped it can be hard to remember which side glass came from which window.

Glass is a big factor in most chops, especially if the car has a curved windshield or back window. These areas can cause more grief that anything else involved in the chop. Cutting glass is an art in itself so, unless you have a lot of skill in this area or know someone that does, get a car with flat glass or get an expert to cut the glass for you. Most shops will not guarantee the cutting of glass. What I do is ask around for "the expert" that does safety glass cutting. I feel a bit more confidant about turning glass over to him.

If the glass is good and you are not chopping the section

This is another technique to hold the filler plate in place as you weld it. The cross piece of aluminum spreads the load of the tube so you will not have a dent on the filler plate from over stressing it in one spot.

The rear filler plate has been run through the English wheel a few times to give it a bit of a curve. You can also see the split rear section of the roof, which will be aligned and welded later.

The door pillar is welded and ground down and ready for any plastic filler that we are going to.

We made a relief cuts above the windshield. This allowed us to spread the "A" pillars apart to meet the bottoms of the same pillars. This will be almost a "metal finish" (no filler) when complete.

The front windshield post is ground down and looks like it will not require much in the way of filler.

The jack is used to adjust the position of the top for welding.

with the curved glass, you should remove the glass and save it in a safe place so you can use it later—if it did not break during the removal, as many do, especially on older cars. Of course, old cars are the hardest to get new glass for. Sometimes the glass is the most expensive part of the car whole project.

A second option to consider is the replacement of glass with a plastic such as "Makrolon," which is a polycarbonate (bullet-resistant) material. It cuts easily with the proper saw blade and can be shaped over an existing piece of glass with a heat gun. Best of all, it will not shatter when you bend it. Some of the plastics have scratch-resistant coatings and some are pre-tinted.

Cutting glass is a black art for most of us. It involves a little chemistry, a little physics, plenty of skill and some luck. It is a frustrating process that will tax your patience. You can be making the final cut in a two-hour job, only

A section of aluminum is added underneath the rear window opening to spread the load as the jack is adjusted.

A sheet of metal is roughed out and placed in position for a first check of the fit. The bottom edge has been turned in 90 degrees and run though a shrinker to add some curve to it.

The top is tack welded in place and ready for total welding after a bit of hammer and dolly work around the edges to straighten out the metal that was warped from the welding.

With the trunk in place, we can begin to see what the finished car will look like.

to see a small crack travel diagonally across what would otherwise be a perfect job.

I would suggest you start by practicing on a similar type of windshield to what you are about to cut for your car. Pick up the cheapest one you can find because it will more than likely get destroyed during the learning process. Old glass cracks much faster and easier than new glass, so start with the old glass to hone your skills. Keep the glass shop's number handy just in case you decide to give up and get an expert to finish the job.

Lay the glass against the car's windshield area, even if it is not the correct windshield, just to simulate the way it is to be done and trace the cut line with a felt tip marker as carefully and slowly as you can making sure that the cut line is exactly the same as the opening in the car's windshield area. You may want to use some of the old windshield gasket or seal and cut a few small sections to slip on the

The upper door sections have to be modified to fit the new roofline.

Now this is a little better! The alignment is made much better just by moving everything forward. The front door post will need to be moved forward. To do this we cut it near the rear so the top could be brought forward.

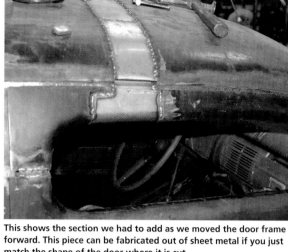

This shows the section we had to add as we moved the door frame forward. This piece can be fabricated out of sheet metal if you just match the shape of the door where it is cut.

The inner frame is extended and welded back together.

Brian works the rear panel to make it flow into the old roof line. He is using a hammer and dolly to bring the high spots down and the low spots up.

Once it is done, it will be impossible to see the patch panel that has replaced the rear window. Later, I will add a rearview camera and monitor.

bottom edge of the glass to help hold it in place and align it with the opening. This will also keep the glass from falling out of place or off the car.

Next, lay the glass on a table padded with a furniture blanket or cardboard and let one edge hang over. Scribe a line with the glass cutter on the previously made felt tip mark, then flip the windshield over and, using a glass cutter, scribe the windshield on the other side directly in line with the same mark. Grab the glass with glass pliers and move it slowly up and down, this will take some practice and this is where the art of glass cutting lies. If the glass starts to crack anywhere other than where you want, stop and try another spot. If all goes well you can now apply a small amount of denatured alcohol to the area you have just cut and light it on fire and let it burn for about 15 to 20 seconds before blowing it out. This should soften the plastic between the glass layers so that it can be easily cut with a razor blade. This will probly take a few hours of practice and you should

Back to the side door tops as we again move around on the car, welding here and there until there is nothing left to weld.

only cut a few inches off at a time. so you will get a lot of practice in trimming the glass down to size. The amount of flex with the pliers and the amount of burn time will determine the outcome of the glass-cutting project.

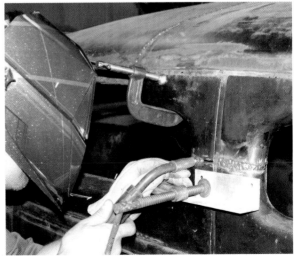

Brian tack welds the rear door window frame in place. Note the use of a clamp and angle to hold the doors in alightment.

Custom Tube Grille

Grilles are nice for keeping birds and small flying rodents out of the radiator and engine compartment, but they should also be an aesthetic enhancement. Most factory grilles are generic in design and stamped out of aluminum or steel in an effort to save a few production bucks over the high cost of bars and tubes. When you customize a car, the grille is quite often the very first thing modified because it's an easy project with an end result that changes the look of a car's front profile dramatically.

It would be totally cool if we could simply come up with a grille design and have it stamped out with a factory fit. The alternative is to purchase an aftermarket grille, but the flooded market of billet grille clones doesn't leave much to the imagination. And that's not what customizing is really about. All it takes to come up with a nice custom grille for any car is a little imagination, a little skill with a welder and a torch, and some metal.

A tube grille is a grille made up of tubes and there is not

This is a custom grille we made for the '72 Mustang project. It is a 1/4-inch steel bar grille with the ends drilled and tapped for plastic rod inserts that will go in the ends and extend over the headlights.

We cut a bunch of the rods and cut male threads on one end of each of them. We radiused the other ends.

much to say about them other than they all basically look the same. Some are horizontal, some vertical, but they are all tube grilles. When I began to plan out the modifications that would be covered in this book, the last thing that I wanted to do was rehash the same old stuff that you see in the car magazines. So when it came to building a custom grille, even though this is a fairly simple modification, I had my work cut out for me to present something unique. Here's what I came up with for the subject vehicle, an early '70s Ford Mustang.

A "phantom" grille is popular among the custom truck crowd today, but the design originated back in the 1960s. The tubes of a phantom grille are horizontal and extend over the headlights. Hiding the lights with the grille creates a phantom effect when the lights are switched on at night.

The design that I came up with is a variation of the phantom grille that uses clear plastic bars on the grille tubes where they extend over the headlights. While making this grille does involve some lathe work, it is a modification that can be done in your garage on a small bench-top lathe/mill machine. These downsized versions of the large production shop machines are easy to operate and fairly affordable. Design-wise, the tubing for the grille will actually consist of 1/4-inch solid steel rod. There are a number of reasons for this, and one is that I planned to incorporate some rather sharp bends in each tube to match the line of the hood and front bumpers. If you've ever tried to put a sharp bend in a hollow tube, you know that it has a tendency to kink and flatten at the bend. Also, the ends of each tube require drilling and tapping for the clear plastic tube extensions. I decided that it would be easier to drill a hole in the end of each rod for just the right tap size, rather than try to match a tap to the diameter of a hollow bar end.

The mounting brackets for the grille must be made before designing the tubes. It can be done the other way around—tubes first—but the chances are greater that you'll run into

Each end was drilled and tapped to accept a plastic rod that would have a threaded end on it. This work can be taken out to a local machine shop.

Next, we made a mounting bracket to hold the grille in place.

The clear grille extension rods are made from Polycarbonate and are very strong, but we made a few extra and then marked which one fit which grille tube as we assembled them. Any of them were designed to fit anyplace, but we marked them anyway.

The ends of the plastic bars were rounded.

Kelly attached the rest of the bars just in time to remove them and send the grille to the chrome platers.

clearance or placement obstacles along the way. Fabricating the mounting bracket for the grille requires some thought. It serves as a mount for the grille tubes, as well as a bracket that must attach securely to the car. The mounting bracket can be flat stock and should run from the radiator core support to the grille, one on the left side and one on the right. Before making any part of the grille, plan ahead or you will wind up with a grille that cannot be removed, or possibly even installed at all.

Once you have brackets that you can bolt onto the car—most likely onto the radiator support, as in the case of our Mustang—you can proceed with the grille tubes by making a sample tube that you can cut, trim, bend and fit onto the brackets. I made a pattern bar that I used to trim and bend until I had the perfect shape. Then I used it for a pattern to make the grille. The pattern bar can be painted red so it does not get mixed up with the grille bars, then

you can also use it to space the grille tubes out evenly while you weld.

Attaching the clear tube extensions to the steel bars is where the lathe work comes in. If you want to drill a hole in the end of several bars and you want each one perfectly centered, you need a lathe, or at least a friend with a lathe. The plastic rods also have to be threaded on the male end. It's possible to hand-drill each of these holes, but consistency will require a lot of careful drilling. You can also take the bars to a machine shop and ask them to thread each bar one inch deep with a 3/8-18 pitch.

The photos that illustrate the grille fabrication include all of the steps that I took to change the look of my Mustang. Keep in mind that your grille will be different, but hopefully you can guide when you apply them to your project.

Custom Hood

The last section of this chapter will show how I modified the hood on two of my cars, the ol' '40 Ford and the '72 Mustang. Chances are, you probably won't get into a hood modification quite this extensive, but most of the techniques that are demonstrated can be used for fabricating a scoop, louver panel or anything similar.

As soon as I got into my hood modification, one thing led to another until the simple welding of the two hood panels on the '40 became a major project in and of itself. As a customizer, I cannot keep it simple. As I perform one task I start thinking of new things to do that will enhance the project even more. This is what happened while welding the '40 hood.

The 1940 Ford, as with many other cars, had a two-piece hood with a seam down the center that was hidden by chrome trim. While this may have been classy in the '40s, it is a bit passé today, so in an effort to bring the car to the age of the new generation, I set about making the hood whole again, or rather, for the first time.

Having the propensity to complicate rather than simplify my mission, I then looked at the car and thought (out loud I might add) that the car now screamed for a tilt-up hood. After all, I could just weld the hood to the front fenders and make the entire unit one piece then tilt it forward. Then Brian asked me, "why forward? Why not backwards?" He had a point! Everyone tilts the hood forward because it is simple, but backwards in not simple, and would require some creative engineering, not to mention a new set of hinges and hydraulics. I love a good challenge so it was a perfect idea and in the process I can also pass the idea on to future customizers.

This hood job was started by adding some 1/4-inch rod to the front edge to give us a guide for the angle we wanted to add to the hood. We also used a flat bar, which we pre-rolled to add a bit of curve to it, as a guide for the shape we wanted.

The bar is moved in 2-inch increments.

As the bar is moved across the hood, the point of contact is marked so we can make a template from the point of contact to the hood.

A sheet of plastic is laid over the hood and the marks transferred to the plastic. The blue is a plastic coating we leave on the sheet for marking.

Two pieces of angle stock are placed along the center line of the hood. The edge of the pattern is then placed flush against the angle for accurate measurement.

The plastic is then trimmed down to the marks that we made earlier, and fit again. We trimmed around the scoop opening as well.

A hammer and dolly are used to bend the flange up around the rod that is welded to the front of the hood. It will later be welded to the rod.

So back to the hood... We started by measuring the length of the seam, then cutting a piece of 3/8-inch-diameter hot-rolled bar stock just about a foot longer than the actual length of the seam. We tacked welded the length of bar onto the seam and, using heat, allowed the bar to contour itself to the hood. Since the hood is a large panel with no structure to reinforce it, we had to be careful with the heating process as well as the welding to avoid warping the metal. Again, we used intermittent stitch welding to minimize heat build-up, keeping the "stitches" no longer than a 1/4 inch long and spaced out by a distance of 4 inches. The stitch welding process takes much longer than running a continuous bead with the welder, but this is time well spent. When we were done, the unsightly seam down the center of the hood was gone and the panel was warp-free.

This is the bottom of the hood extension after it was partially welded in place.

The hood is welded up and we have laid a bent bar down for the angle of the grille. It was bent to the angle of the hood as we were making the hood.

The bumpers are on and a front flare started. The cardboard is covering the windshield to protect it from sparks that would ruin the glass.

The welds are ground down and the hood is ready for the body shop.

The custom grille and hood finish off the front end very nicely, giving the "Frankenstang" a nice nose job.

This hood of the 1940 Ford had some rust issues. The first thing we needed to do before beading it was to remove the rust under where the bar (for the bead) was to be welded.

We even tried the wire brush on it, but this still did not get inside the seam. A small course-grit grinding wheel was used to remove most of the rust.

The rod was TIG welded from the front toward the back and, in this case, we wanted the heat to build up so we could bend the rod as we went along.

We were heating, bending and welding as we moved along.

The bar was almost flat as we switched to a MIG welder for a bit more speed.

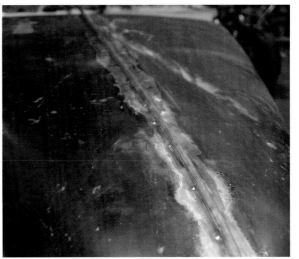

The rod was welded in some spots just to hold the rod in place. It will later receive the finish welds.

Chapter Five

More Modifications—Customizing Tricks for Cars Both Old and New

You may remember the Supra used in both *The Fast and The Furious* (orange then) and *2Fast 2Furious* (gold now). We put that car together in about four days. Most of the stuff was just a bolt-on kit. The hardest part was the paint.

We also built a Tiburon that sported custom ground effects all the way around. The aftermarket hood was made of carbon fiber and the suspension was an air cylinder system that allowed us to lower the car to the ground.

Ground Effects
3-D "Speed" Grille

Thanks in part to movies like *The Fast and the Furious* and its sequel *2Fast 2Furious*. "Tuner" cars are all the rage these days. And no tuner car would be "in tune" without a fancy bolt-on set of ground effects. Ground effects are all part of a body kit that consists of a front air dam/bumper cover, side rocker panels, and a rear bumper cover. The style of ground effects can vary from mild to extremely wild, but one thing that most kits have in common is an abundance of air scoops and streamlined looking ducts that, whether fake or functional, exude a look of speed.

Some of the body kit manufacturers provide a flexible mesh material for this purpose that the installer must cut to fit. Whenever we install ground effects here at Customs By Eddie Paul, this part of the kit goes straight into the dumpster. The main reason is that the mesh that comes with most kits looks like chicken wire and is much too flexible. Flexibility makes it easy to install, but the material is so soft that it's easily damaged.

My solution to this dilemma is to, you guessed it, fabricate our own using a better-looking and more durable mesh material. You can use any number of materials to build these "grilles" for your ground effects, or even use the material that came with your kit if you so desire. When it comes time for installation, though, it's not as plain and

More Modifications—Customizing Tricks for Cars Both Old and New

Installing grilles over the vents and openings on aftermarket ground effects is optional. Usually, installing the grilles gives a finished look, such as on this Eclipse.

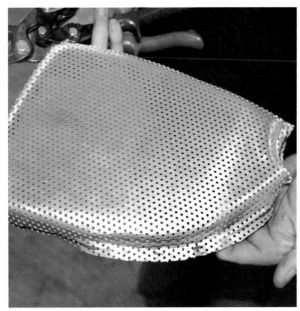

Scoop opening screens are normally just a flat piece of screen glued in the opening of a scoop. But with a little effort, and a bit of skill, you can make them look as if they were built in an automotive plant.

I was walking through my shop when we were building the cars for "2F2F" and saw one of my guys sitting on the concrete floor looking like he was doing nothing. Well, my payroll alarm went off and I so I politely asked him "what are you doing sitting there?" to which he responded "I'm holding the screen in place while the epoxy cures," which is what the body kit manufacturer recommended in its instructions. "How long have you been sitting there I asked?" his response, "I don't know about an hour, I think…"

To me, this can be compared to watching paint dry, or grass grow. Sitting is definitely not productive, and I looked at a few kits we had from the manufactures and noticed most of the screens were glued in with some sort of adhesive. This just didn't look right. In fact, it was really just a makeshift method that would not last. So I invented a better and simpler way to install the screens that requires a minimum of skill in woodworking, a few tools and a couple of hours, probably as long as it would take to watch that glue set up. An added benefit is that the screens will be removable.

You can start by holding a block of pattern wood or even a piece of pine up to the scoop opening and, with a pencil, mark the shape of the opening onto the wood. This will leave you with an outline of the scoop opening to cut out

simple as you might expect. The problem is not with the screen material, but with finding a good way to anchor it to the body. The screen material can be easily "formed" by hand to give it shape and depth, not only increasing its appeal, but adding strength to an otherwise flat screen. We have found a simple way to shape the screens that almost anyone can do with a piece of wood a soft hammer and a chunk of expanded metal (screen).

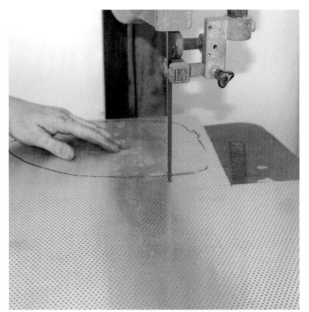

First pick out a screen design that you like out of aluminum. Design ideas can be found on the web or may come with a kit. You can trim the design to the size you need to work with.

Cut a plywood pattern (male plug) of the hole size you need to fill with a screen and radius the edges of the male plug with a router.

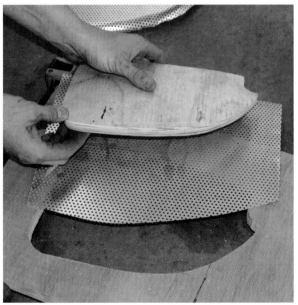

Save the section of wood that you cut the male plug out of. This will be the female part of the form used to form a screen. The male plug should fit inside the female form with just about a saw blade-width space around it allowing for the screen thickness.

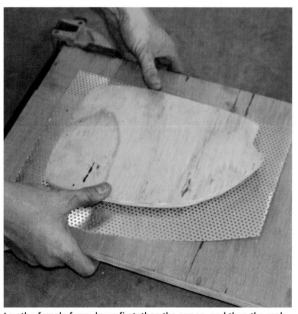

Lay the female form down first, then the screen, and then the male plug in alignment.

of the wood. The wood should be about 6 inches larger than the opening in all directions, allowing the outline part of the wood to be used for the pressing of the outer edge of the screen. A saber saw is used to cut the center piece out of the pattern; a pilot hole will need to be drilled for the saw blade to avoid sawing through the outline of the wood. Try to drill the pilot hole and start the cut as close as possible to the outline because both pieces of the wood will be used to shape the screen.

Take the inner piece of wood and radius (round off) the outer edges. This piece of the wood will serve as the "stamp" that will press the screen into the wood outline to form the shape of the scoop. Rounding off the edges of the

stamp will add to the strength and looks of the soon-to-be-finished screen. The larger you make the radius, the better the screen will look—in my opinion.

Once the inner wood stamp is radiused, take the piece of expanded aluminum mesh—either the one that came with your body kit, or a piece of mesh that you've selected—and place it over the wood outline (the part with the opening cut out of the center) and place the stamp (with the radiused edges down toward the screen). Press the dies together to shape the screen. If the mesh material that you've chosen is difficult to press, C-clamps will provide the added leverage to do this.

Once the wooden "dies" are pressed flat, they can be

The edges will be a bit wrinkled, but these can easily be repaired and most of the edges will be trimmed away in the fitting process.

Now, using an arbor press, or large clamp, squeeze the three parts together forcing the mail plug into he female form. This will give the screen a 3-D form.

Try a test fit of the screen in the opening and note the areas that need to be trimmed or tweaked.

separated and the screen removed. If you've centered the mesh and pressed it evenly, you'll notice that it has a flange around the outer edge. This part of the mesh can be trimmed to a constant width and will serve as the mounting flange for the screen. Be sure to save the wooden dies so you can remake the screens for yourself or your friends who have the same body kit. The final step to this project is optional. You can paint the mesh inserts to match or complement your paint job, or you can change them to flat black for a competition look.

The screen is trimmed and tested in the opening as many times as necessary until you have a perfect fit.

Eddie Paul's Custom Bodywork Handbook

Our electric window kit came from Electric-Life and was very simple to install into a car that never had power windows. In fact, the whole job was done in less than a day. Electric-Life offers three different kits and each provides up to roughly 20 inches of window lift.

Electric Window Conversion

I had just finished the six cars for the movie *xXx* (that's "Triple X", not *rated* X!) and as is the norm, I overestimated how many cars the studio wanted. This happens to me more than you would think, and I was stuck with a pretty nice 1967 GTO. Poor me! In any event, I realized that my daughter, who was about 10 years old at the time, had never ridden in a real muscle car before, so I asked her if she wanted to go for a ride.

Being a "T-type" personality, she jumped in without question and said, "only if we can go real fast!" to which I agreed. Now, I would not race with Ariel in the car, and I do not race on the streets anyway, but her idea of going fast is a rapid take off, which I could accommodate her on without even spinning the tires!

But before I could take off, she stopped me as she stared toward her door, and asked, "What is that?" She was pointing at the door panel as if there was a giant spider crawling on

it. I quickly pulled over not knowing exactly what it was. She pointed again, *at the window crank handle!*

I was still confused when it hit me: She had never seen a window crank handle before! All she ever saw up until this moment were the power window switches in our late-model cars. So I told her to turn the crank and see what happens.

The rest of her first ride in a classic muscle car was spent cranking that window up and down, a feature she thought was "totally cool!" The part about riding in a GTO rated a very distant second to her. What really etched this amusing little episode forever in my mind was when we got back, she looked over at me with her big brown eyes and asked if it was a new invention, and if we could have them put on all our cars.

Which brings us back to the subject of power window conversion, manual-to-power that is. There are enough conversion kits on the market today that manufacturers focus on ease of installation. The days of complex

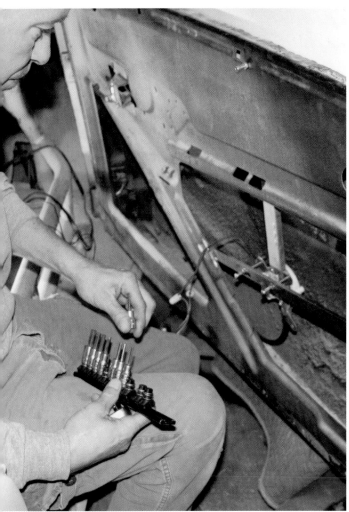

We ran a support brace across the inner door opening to have something to attach to, and used extra-long bolts with double nuts so the window regulator could be simply adjusted.

This shot shows the method that we used for alignment. The long bolt was later swapped out for the proper-length bolt and spacer just by measuring the existing "set-up" bolts.

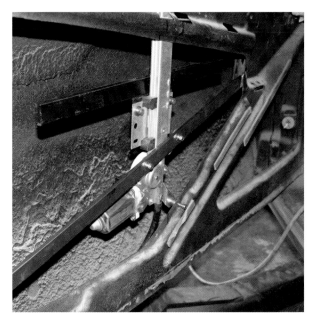

The horizontal glass sash is ready to be cleaned and siliconed into place.

mechanisms with parallelograms and levers and greasy gears long gone. You can now buy a universal window conversion kit that you can install with minimal effort in almost any car within a day.

Power Windows, Step By Step

- Remove everything that is in the way of your windows, such as the door panels and insulation, as well as the sticky tar that sometimes holds it in place. This will save you the aggravation of getting it all over yourself each time you reach in the window. As you remove each part of the window, tag it and bag it so you will be able to find it later. We often put the parts in the trunk of the car we are working on just so we know where they are when we need a screw or bolt that only fits in one place. I cannot emphasize enough that the more organized you are, the faster you can perform a task, whether you're doing it in a shop or in your garage.

- Make a template using the old window for a guide if you have to have one cut to fit the car especially. This will definitely be necessary if you have chopped the top and the stock window will no longer fit. We often make a glass pattern out of Makrolon so it can be drilled or cut and will not break easily. Then the glass cutter can use this for the template for the new glass.

- Way back when, I used to have to steal an electric window out of other cars, such as a Cadillac, and this was not easy task. They were designed to work in Cadillacs, not Chevrolets. Now, many companies have simple universal kits that really do "fit anything." They are relatively cheap and simple to install and seem to work well. We tried a few of them to see for ourselves if the ad was correct, and after only a few hours we had

Eddie Paul's Custom Bodywork Handbook

A bubble level will help keep the window in proper alignment. Alignment is very important for making the window open and close properly.

electric windows.

➤ Hold the mechanism in the door and see what you need in the way of mounting brackets. This way you can determine the amount of lift and the location of the drive motor, and you can also see where the mounting brackets need to be connected on the door frame. You will also be able to determine the routing of the wiring for the buttons as well as the door window butting location.

➤ Hold the window mechanism up to the door and check the window travel to see how much of the track has to be trimmed down. Most of the kits include a track that is much longer than you will need and is meant to be trimmed to fit the window travel of your car. Using a square or level, or both, hold the track perpendicular to the base of the window frame and hold the window mechanism up so you can mark the area that the mounting brackets need to be located.

➤ With this information you can now fabricate your mounting brackets that will attach from the mechanism to the inner door panel. This bracket should be made form metal of the same gauge as the door panel. There

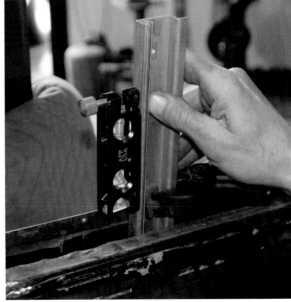

The vertical channel is held up to the window to see how much should be cut off to allow the mechanism to fit in the door. These are made long and can be shortened to fit.

More Modifications—Customizing Tricks for Cars Both Old and New

This is the "AWSOM 50" from the movie *Cobra*. We installed electric windows as we restored the car to show condition for Robert Bennett. Here, his girlfriend Julie is testing the window for strength.

We kept the inside simple, with only a door latch and a button for the control of the one window. The inner door panel was a 6061-T6 aluminum panel with a single bead running around the perimeter.

are normally a few mounting locations that you can choose from, just pick the one that is the closest to the mechanism to eliminate as much flex in the mounting bracket as possible.

► Test fit the bracket by bolting it in place. For this you can use longer bolts and extra nuts to give you the ability to adjust and align the glass as it travels up and down in the "C" channel. Once the distance is determined, the longer bolts and nuts can be replaced with the correct bolts and a set of spacers made from tubing.

► Once the mechanism is in and adjusted, you may want to replace the old "C" channel with a new one-piece "C" channel. These can be purchased in lengths of about 4 feet and then trimmed down to whatever you need. You will also need the felt that goes inside the channel. It is normally sold at the same place as the channel. If the window is working well and the channel has been replaced you are about done with the electric conversion, but just to be sure recheck the bolts and be sure that they are all tight and that you have installed lock washers or Lock Tight to each of them.

Split Windshield

The split windshield how-to is a design-specific modification that may or may not work on your car. After all, a windshield is not something you probably give a lot of thought to…unless you're like me.

The first windshield didn't appear until about 1919 when the first piece of cut plate glass was added to the dash area of a car to do nothing more than eliminate the need to wear goggles, which were the only thing keeping the bugs and dust out of the driver's eyes. As cars began to go a little faster, the need for a windshield became more and more evident and the focus was directed toward the looks of the windshield and how to make it more streamlined as well as how to keep it clear. This prompted Studebaker to unveil the first windshield wiper in 1938. The now-defunct auto manufacturer Kaiser offered a pop-out windshield and, in '39, Dodge was the first to introduce a curved glass windshield that revolutionized automotive glass design.

So in a nutshell, we have come from flat glass, to split flat glass, to curved one-piece glass. Now I am taking

From the front you can see the complete "AWSOM 50" project and the rubber molding that has been installed around the windshield, as well as the center rubber.

This is the 1940 Ford just after the top was chopped a whopping 6 inches. I hated the thought of putting the stock windshield splitter bar back in and I came up with another new idea.

The first step was to grind the metal in the area that I planned to work. This was performed with a small air grinder.

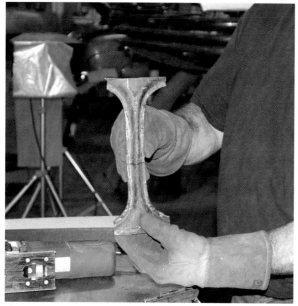

The rear section of widow is taken to the workbench and cut down to a smaller size for ease of fit. All the outer section was removed and we are left with an "I" beam center section that was trimmed for height. Six inches were removed from the center so that it would fit in the windshield area. Actually, it was a bit less than 6 inches, as the post is at a slight angle.

The two parts are held roughly in their new home and checked for fit again.

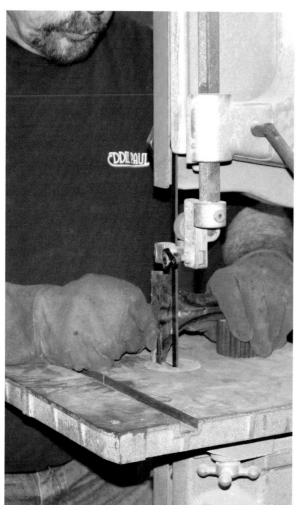

I then took off the inner area that interfered with the fit to the car's windshield area. This is a slow process of fitting and trimming one spot at a time until the part fits perfectly.

the concept full circle by going back to a split-flat glass windshield on my '40, but with a touch more style than the original chrome metal bar.

When I chopped the top a somewhat radical 6 inches, I found the back window had nowhere to fit, so I carefully put it aside for future use. As I was looking at the hood and the bead we added, it seemed that the bead needed to go somewhere and that we could add the back window divide to the front windshield and run the bead up the divide as a gusset.

This is what customizing is all about: an idea pops in your head and you run with it and then it leads to another idea. But the car was coming together quite nicely and it is starting to draw crowds as we worked into the night, cutting and welding, bending and bonding, chopping and frenching. This former rust bucket was coming back to life, and we were adding a shot of adrenalin to kick its heart into rhythm.

With all the work going into the '40, this was a good point to stop and go to the sandblaster rust removal by abrasive blasting. This step would give me an idea of where the metal would have to be spliced between the old and the new. Blasting will all but remove the seriously rusted metal and only etch the sound metal.

I purposely waited until this point to blast as much of the rusty metal was going to be cut away anyway, and there was no need to spend time and money blasting metal I was going to cut away. Also, it is easier to get to some of the seams once the floor is cut out and badly rusted parts removed.

I measured the area from the rear window to see what I needed from it and this wound up being a very small section but one that would otherwise be hard to fabricate from scratch. I also grabbed my video camera and performed a quick introduction for my next How-To video on customizing and made a commitment to how long I thought the whole process would take from concept to completion; this time I stated two hours! The whole process

I may grind, cut or bend to get the perfect fit and then repeat the process after a trial fit. Never rush the process until you are 100 percent satisfied with the fit.

The rear section of this divider was removed so it would clear the dash area. I could have just as well removed the dash area, but this was the easier of the two to modify.

was one and a half hours, but I had to stop for photos as well as video so the entire job was actually finished in about one hour.

The center divider was the only thing I saved from the back window. This was shaped like a capital "I". I then slit it across the center of the main pillar to make two separate pieces, the top and the bottom. The part would have to be split anyway, and this made it much easier to deal with as two separate pieces, rather than one. The most difficult part was not the cutting or welding, or even the alignment of the edges of the two separate parts; it was finding the center of the windshield. The big problem was that it was just out of reach from the outside of the car and we had to lean way over to reach it. I knew I should have channeled the car first. The other problem was that there was no real crease in the center of the roof or bottom of the windshield, only a suggested peak. And to add more to the mix, the whole car is rounded and there is not an outside vertical section to use as a datum point for reference of measurement. It is somewhat like trying to draw a centerline on a basketball; it can be done but, wow, what a pain. We even tried a laser

I then started working with the top section alone to make sure it fit, then I moved to the bottom section. Breaking the job into two sections makes things easier.

As soon as it looked as if I was close to having it fit, I put the section in a vise and tapped the center area, forming it into a slight "V" shape to match the centerline "V" of the roof. The felt tip mark for the center of the part is where I tapped it with a chisel-tipped hammer.

Now the fun part of the job—finding the centerline of the roof at the windshield area. It's not unlike finding the center of a ball, but with the aid of an antenna hole and a center hole in the dash (complements of Ford), I only had to add a piece of tape as a more visible reference for the center.

OK, so it was not the last fit, but the top piece is in and I am working on the bottom now.

off the center peak of the hood; to no avail. You still need a reference to start the vertical line off of, and basketballs have no vertical lines.

Finally I relied on Henry Ford's original design for the answer. After all, he built the car and I can only assume he put the roof antenna in the true center of the windshield so this was now our one and only center line reference point. From here we simply ran a piece of rod down through the shaft and drove it into the hole in the top of the dash where

the old radio antenna had been.

Now we had a center! From here on it was smooth sailing, as I put the already-cut top piece of the divider into place and marked and trimmed it with the car's body until the top part of the divider slid into perfect alignment with the windshield flanges (where the glass molding attaches), then Brian would get back and give it the "Japanese eye test" for a final alignment (his eyes are calibrated horizontally to within about one-ten-thousandth of an inch, while mine

The dash had to be cut back slightly at the center for the bottom divider to fit, but this only took a few minutes.

The bottom section is slid in place next to the top piece and marked for length and cutting on the band saw.

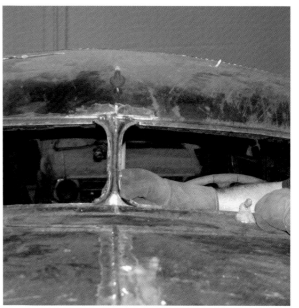

The bottom section slides in as if it were made for the windshield.

are not), and as soon as he said "go!" I let the sparks fly as I added the first tack weld, making the two pieces one. The other half, or bottom of the windshield post, was simple to add. We just aligned it to the top section and cut and sliced until it fit and looked good. Then it was time to weld it into place, grind the weld smooth, and it was ready to be metal worked to a smooth finish.

In keeping with the "round theme" of this car I decided to add a filler plate under the gusset which would be a simple plate of metal with three holes drilled in it. The reason for three is that it is artistically pleasing. Odd numbers for some strange reason are pleasing, not even numbers. I try to stick with the number three whenever I design something. I guess two is a balance and three is not? In any event, I will have three holes on the gusset and three taillights as well as three antennas, and three runningboard bars.

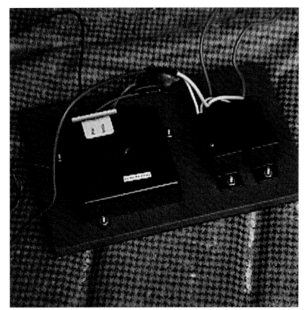

We mounted the keyless entry module (one receiver) and the two solenoids onto a board for mounting in the trunk area on the *xXx* GTO.

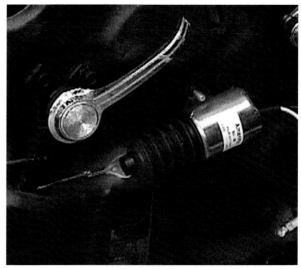

On the *xXx* GTO, we mounted the door solenoids on the cabin side panel of the door because the production company wanted to have gadgets everywhere. This added to the "junk" in the car, but we would normally hide the solenoid behind the door panel, so it is not seen. We hooked it up using a cable.

This is the muscle of the kit, the solenoid. It will pull most door handles with ease, but when you install it make sure you have the right ratio for a good solid pull on a lever. The solenoid has a set amount of travel and a set amount of force, so if you shorten its pull by half (moving it closer to the pivot point of the lever), you will double its load requirement or needed strength. You will probably need to play with the ratio of the pull.

Electric Door Conversion

Converting your door latches to operate with an electric solenoid is one of those age-old custom tricks that never seems to get old. Sometimes referred to as "shaving the doors" or "solenoid doors," the electric door conversion is an easy modification that substitutes the outer door handle mechanism for a concealed solenoid linkage. It can be performed on any car. Most are easy, some hard due to limited space or interference with existing hardware. Once the solenoid linkage is installed, the outer door handle and key lock are removed and the holes in the door skin are welded up and smoothed, leaving no trace of how driver and passenger can open the doors to enter the vehicle.

Shaving the door handles, especially on older cars where the handle was an obtrusive piece of hardware, is a way to really clean up the side of a car. If the idea intrigues

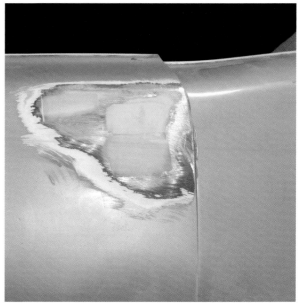

We shaved the door handles on the cars by removing the handle and welding a small piece of metal to fill the remaining hole left by the now missing door handle. After the welding, we simply filled in the low spots with body filler and got the door ready for primer.

you and you're wondering how this works, you'll have to remove the interior door panel to familiarize yourself with the latch mechanism. Basically, both the outer and inner door handles are connected to the latch via a rod with one or more pivot points. Pressing or pulling on the handle pulls the rod to release the latch from the striker. The power conversion simply eliminates the outer handle by connecting the rod directly to the push-pull arm of a solenoid.

The electric door idea has been around for quite a while and the most common solenoid device used in the conversion is a standard heavy-duty 12-volt push-pull solenoid typically found in a car's starting system. What

A door jammer's sole purpose in life is to pop your door open when you hit the button to the remote door opener. It simply gets mounted in the door hinge area and uses a very strong spring that pushes the door open from the hinge area.

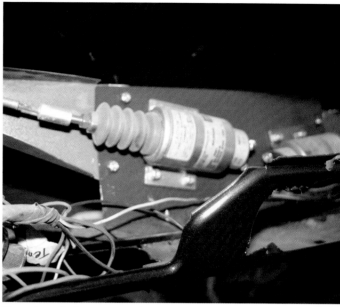

We made a sub plate to mount the solenoids to under the dash and threaded the ends of the solenoids to accept the threaded cable ends. The cables were from a surplus store and were some type of aircraft control cable. They cost about $1 each.

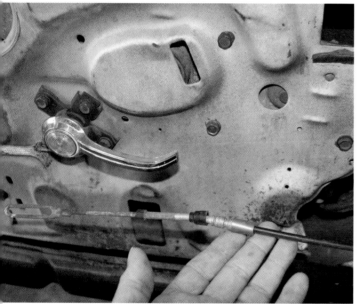

This is the end of cable that I am running through the door hinge to the door latch, from the solenoids under the dash.

Removing the door handles helped make the *xXx* GTO a very smooth car.

has changed in recent years is the mode of activating the solenoid. A hard-wired button switch controls the solenoid from some hidden location on the car, but solenoid systems are now capable of wireless operation from a remote key fob switch.

I once heard of a guy that shaved his door handles and used a remote switch that would only actuate the solenoid when a certain sequence of buttons were pushed in a certain amount of time. The guy had a slight drinking problem and it was his way of not driving under the influence. This sure sounds like an idea for a patent, but in any case, the removal of the door handle and key is pretty straight forward and the cutting of a pattern for the metal that will fill the hole in the door requires basic fabrication techniques that you can find elsewhere in this book.

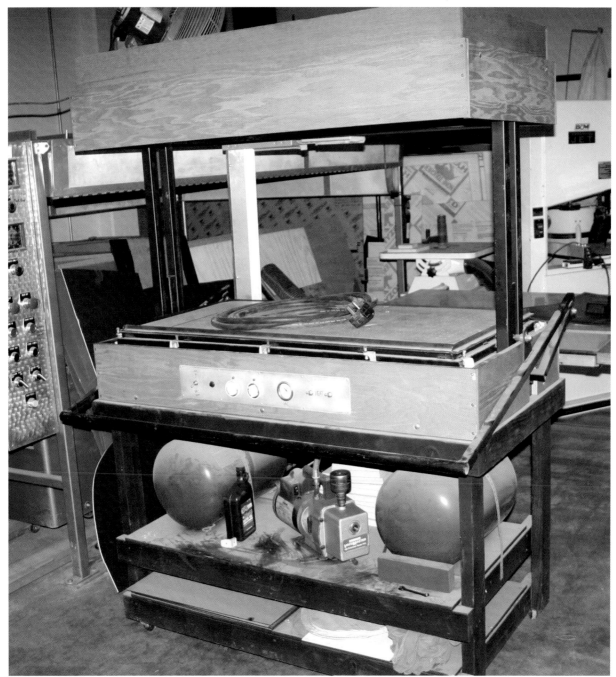

This vacuum-forming machine was assembled from a set of plans that I purchased from Special Effects Supply Company for $120.

Vacuum-forming Machines

The process of vacuum-forming can open up a whole new world of things that can be fabricated for automotive use. This was covered briefly in Chapter Three. Without vacuum-forming, I would never have made the deadline for the filming of the movie *Taxi*. But you don't have to be mass-producing body kits for a Crown Victoria to make use of this form of customizing; there are numerous practical applications for working with plastic. So much so that I have two vacuum-forming machines in my shop that my crew and I use all the time.

One of my favorite tools, the vacuum-forming machine

is versatile, cost-effective and easy to use. There is one not-so-minor drawback, however: a machine that will form an 8 x 4-foot sheet of plastic will set you back about 20 grand. This, of course, is a full-on industrial-sized unit with all the bells and whistles. If you're really interested in the process of vacuum-forming on a hobbyist scale, there's a much cheaper alternative: You can build one from a kit for less than a grand. These smaller versions work just as well as the big ones since most parts that you would vacuum-form can be fabricated from a quarter sheet (2 x 4 feet) of plastic.

Vacuum-forming machines, whether large or small, are easy to use and can produce one or many copies of a

A set of covers were vacuum formed from black ABS plastic. Several different parts can be formed in one process with the machine at left.

Parts formed from ABS look good and require a simple trim to fit. This piece conceals the trunk latch mechanism on the '50 Merc.

part from a single "plug" (a wooden shape that you make around which the plastic is formed). The process is simple enough and the cost of the machine can vary depending on how much of the machine you're willing to build yourself. You can make battery trays, air dams, glove compartment liners, hood scoops, trim pieces, dash parts or even body parts if the machine is large enough. The best and easiest plastic to use is common ABS (acrylonitrile-butadiene-styrene—no wonder we call it ABS!) which is available in several colors. Some plastic suppliers have an array of custom colors and simulated textures such as carbon fiber, marble and wood that can be special-ordered. Acrylics (Plexiglas) and polycarbonates (Makrolon, Lexan) also can be formed for parts such as lenses, dashboard gauge panels, compound curved windows, etc.

Most plastics are thermally formable—able to be shaped when heat is applied—and can be heated to a formable point with a standard heat gun or even an electric heater. The biggest trick in vacuum forming is making the "plug" that will determine the shape and fit of the finished part. All of your attention to design and detail should go into the making of the plug just as it would with fabricating with sheet metal.

The concept of vacuum-forming is fairly straightforward. A sheet of plastic is heated to a point beyond normal flexibility but less than its melting point. While at its soft formable stage, the plastic is pulled down over a mold and a burst of air suction pulls the softened plastic tightly around the shape of the mold. When the plastic cools, it will then take on the new shape provided by the mold.

There are only a couple of potential mistakes to avoid in the process. The first involves heating the plastic. If the sheet of plastic is overheated, obviously it will melt. If not enough heat is applied, the plastic will not totally conform to the shape of the mold. Actually, the heat range in which

When building your own vacuum-forming machine, make sure to get a good pump. The one on my machine is a 1/2-hp Robinair Vacumaster.

the plastic is workable is quite forgiving and with a couple of trial-and-error attempts, you should be able to cast a good part.

Another mistake to avoid involves the shape of the plug. Since the plastic will be vacuum-formed very tightly around the mold, you must be able to remove it from the formed plastic once it has cooled. This is where most people get stumped.

A common mistake made by beginners and experienced vacuum formers alike is to make a plug that cannot be removed from the newly formed plastic. You *must* be able to remove your plug from the plastic after it forms around the plug! In order to remove the plug from the formed plastic,

A 2 x 4-foot sheet allowed us to make four parts at one time for *The Fast and The Furious* Supra.

the shape of the plug must have sufficient "draft." Draft is a term that refers to the shape of the plug in relation to the shape of the plastic that is formed around it.

Good woodworking techniques and tools are needed for successful vacuum-forming, since the plug will usually be made of wood. The wooden plug must be shaped to the exact dimensions required for the part and the finish of the wooden plug must be as smooth as possible. After shaping, it should be sanded with progressively finer sandpaper grits. Final sanding should be done with a 320-grit paper. Follow this with a few coats of wood primer, let it dry, then wax the part a few times. Finishing the plug in this way will make it easier to remove it from the formed plastic.

Once you have a good plug, you will need to cut some plastic for the forming process. The size should be about 6 to 12 inches larger around the shape of the plug. Then make a frame from 1 x 2-inch pine, anchoring it at the corners with screws or nails, and then staple the plastic to the frame, making it look somewhat like a picture frame. Use a thin (1/16 inch) sheet of plastic to start with and then work up to thicker sheets later as you learn more about the technique. The thinner plastic will be easier to remove if something goes wrong.

If you look at the components of a vacuum-forming machine, you'll see how simple the system is. An industrial-sized machine will have a bank of heating elements built into the upper framework to heat the plastic and these require mega-amperage to operate. The lower section will consist of a vacuum platform made of sheet aluminum. The platform is evenly perforated with tiny holes spaced about a quarter inch apart across the entire surface. Underneath this platform is a plenum chamber that directs the vacuum from the air storage tank to the perforated platform. You can find perforated metal at most metal supply companies to make a platform. The platform must lay on a frame made into a hollow box with the perforated screen being the top surface and have supports every few inches apart to support the table top. Another way to get the same effect is to simply lay a screen down covering the vacuum hole and place your part over the screen. The reason for this screen is so the plug does not interfere or block the flow of vacuum.

A sliding fixture that will securely hold a sheet of plastic is also part of the framework. The fixture must slide up to expose the plastic sheet to the heating elements, and then slide down onto the vacuum platform. When a heated

The Supra in *2Fast 2Furious* had one of my plastic inserts designed just for this car. It has since started a trend.

sheet of plastic is lowered down to the platform, it will stretch over the plug. When the vacuum in the tank is released, the suction pulls the softened plastic tightly over the plug thereby replicating the shape of the plug down to the smallest detail.

The actual process of vacuum forming takes just a few seconds if the machine is functioning properly. Closed-cell foam weather-stripping whould be used around all seams to prevent vacuum leaks (open-cell foam does not make an air-tight seal).

Heating the sheet of plastic to the right temperature depends on the type of plastic used. Ideally, you want to heat the plastic to the point that it becomes soft and pliable, almost like pizza dough. For those of you who've never tossed a pizza, the plastic should be hot enough to fold easily, but not at a point of melting. After forming your part, the plastic must cool to the touch, then you can remove the plug and use it again whenever you want to form another part.

This rear shot shows the look of the final NSX modification. The first one was the most expensive because we had to make the tooling, but after that they were rather inexpensive to produce.

Bed Your Glass

OK, so you've chopped the top and you're ready to fit the glass back in. You paid an arm and a leg to have your windows custom cut to the new chopped dimensions, only to find out that one of them doesn't quite fit! What now?

If you find yourself in this predicament, you're not alone. With customizing comes unforeseen setbacks, and few tops ever get chopped without having to deal with ones like this.

Whenever you perform extensive surgery on the roof of a vehicle, whether it be a top chop or a repair, the channel, or "bed" around the window opening that the glass fits

into, must match the contour of the glass precisely. If it doesn't, you stand a chance of breaking the glass during installation. We did a major repair on a chopped 1950 Merc that was rolled over onto its roof. The aftermath of the accident wasn't quite as devastating as it would have been since the Merc had a full roll cage inside. Still, the damage was substantial, concentrated on the right rear section of the roof.

To make a long story short, the damage was repaired, except for the rear window opening, which was irreparable. Most of the bed where the glass fits into had to be cut away and the small section that was left was badly rippled. When

The rear window of the Merc was a bit on the edgy side when we got the car back for restoration. With rust removed and replaced with steel rods the edge was strong enough to work with.

Everglass was mixed just like regular body filler, using a small piece of wood as a palette. Everglass is reinforced with fiberglass strands for extra strength.

We covered the rear window with clear plastic wrap, taped in place, and applied a liberal amount of filler to the edges where the glass met the window opening shelf. You can see the filler around the bottom edge.

Once the window is in place, you can fill a bit around the edges to make an edge for the window to set into.

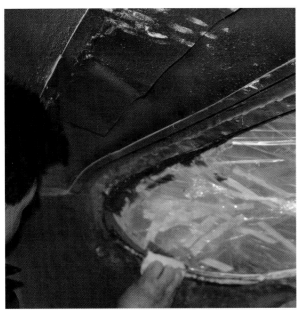

We wipe outward toward the outer fender of the car so the Everglass can be pressed in deep, filling the gap between the glass and the window trough.

It will take two people to lift the window out easily without taking a chance of breaking it. This will have to be performed a number of times, so don't tackle this job without a friend around to help.

This gives you an idea of what the rear window looks like after making a cast with the Everglass against the glass (wrapped in plastic cling wrap). You can see the wrinkles from the plastic, but the basic shape is that of the window.

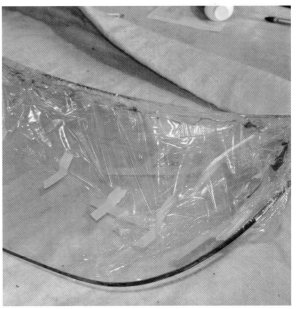

The rear window is removed, cleaned and rewrapped for the next cast (bedding). This process may take as many as five or six tries to get the rear window to fit perfectly, so be patient.

it came time to trial-fit the rear window, we discovered that the glass was only touching the bed in three small spots. Whether a rubber molding will hold the window in place, or the glass is to be sealed directly into the bed with caulking, the glass must contact the bed evenly all the way around. If one small peak sticks up too high, the weight of the glass alone can cause it to break.

And then there's the issue of leakage. We definitely had a problem to solve with this one. If this were a more common later-model car, we could have tracked down a salvaged body for its rear roof section and crafted it into place. This wasn't an option with a customized '50 Merc.

We had two options remaining: We could spend the time to fabricate the entire rear roof section and make a new window opening (very time-consuming and expensive to the owner), or we could work with the existing metal on the car and "bed" the glass.

Bedding is what a good gunsmith does to custom-fit the barrel into the wooden stock of a target rifle. He gets the channel as close as possible by carving and filing, then uses the process of bedding to attain a perfect fit. The bedding of a gun barrel involves resins and wood. The bedding of a car window is done with metal and plastic body filler. If you know how to work with metal and fillers, it's possible

Working With Plastic Body Filler

Most car guys refer to plastic body filler as "Bondo." Bondo is actually a trademark name of Dynatron. While I'm sure that Dynatron products work well, the type of plastic body filler that I use in my shop is made by Evercoat. The system of fillers and undercoatings that Evercoat manufactures is quite extensive; each type of filler and primer is formulated to meet specific applications or to enhance certain qualities to make bodywork easier and longer lasting. The following are the Evercoat products that my shop uses for work on metal-bodied vehicles:

- Rage Xtreme and Z-Grip: polyester filler for repairs and light molding
- Everglass: glass-reinforced filler for repairs and molding with exposure to moisture
- Metal2Metal: metal-reinforced filler for high-strength and rust-prone areas
- Metal Glaze: self-leveling filler for final skim coat over heavy sanding marks and pinholes
- Fiber Tech; glass-reinforced filler for bonding and repairing fiberglass
- Acid Etch Primer: self-etching primer for bare metal
- Featherfill: catalyzed high-solids polyester primer
- Slick Sand: catalyzed extra high-build primer

It's a general misconception that plastic fillers do not last. And it's a direct result of improper use when evidence of plastic filler use can be seen after the car is painted. When a surface has been properly prepared and a filler is mixed and applied correctly, it will last the life of the car.

It's nice if you can afford the time to hammer, shrink and roll a panel and metal-finish it with no use of filler. But in the real world, good-quality plastic fillers and undercoatings play an important role in customizing and body repair. True metal finishing is an antiquated art. It's something to strive for, but learning how to work with plastic body filler is one of the most practical and useful techniques to acquire.

Between castings, shape the edge and trim down the excess that has built up.

The first thing that we had to do was to fabricate some kind of permanent ledge around the window opening onto which we could perform the bedding. As I mentioned earlier, all we had to work with was about 12 inches of window channel in the opening. So to create a bed, we duplicated the shape of the window opening slightly smaller than the actual diameter using 1/4-inch mild steel bar stock. The 1/4-inch bar stock is strong, yet easy enough to make the gradual bends by hand. Once the framework matched the shape of the window opening, we welded it into place with a small 110-volt MIG welder. This is a step that few people will ever have to go through to bed a window. In most cases, the window channel will only be a tad out of shape, rather than totally non-existent as with this Merc.

With a ledge in place, all metal in and around the window channel must be degreased and ground down to expose bare shiny metal. This is the critical step that determines how strong the filler bond will be and how long it will last. Plastic body filler must not be applied over old paint, primer, rust or dirty metal.

At this point the window glass is ready to be bedded. Before mixing up your filler, you must have the glass ready to form the bed. The window itself will be used to create the shape of the bed, just as a gunsmith uses the barrel to shape his wooden rifle stock. To protect the glass, we placed it on a padded surface, then wrapped it with cellophane, making sure that no part of the window glass, especially around the edges, could come into contact with the filler. The cellophane also acts as a mold release, allowing the window to be lifted out after it is pressed into the filler.

Step two is to lay the glass into place, making sure that it sits flush with an even gap around the perimeter of the window. You may want to make plastic shims to insert in between the glass and the shelf to hold the glass at the proper level until the bedding is made.

to bed a rear window in a few short hours. But this isn't a commonly acquired skill, so chances are, if you're bedding your glass, it'll probably be your first and only time so I recommend that you take as much time as you need and get totally familiar with the materials and techniques involved. When we started to bed the glass in the '50 Merc, all of the bodywork was complete and otherwise ready to prepare for painting. Discovering the problem with the rear window required us to take a few steps back to make the necessary repairs to bed the glass.

The near-finished rear window area is primed and sanded and almost ready for the glass to be installed.

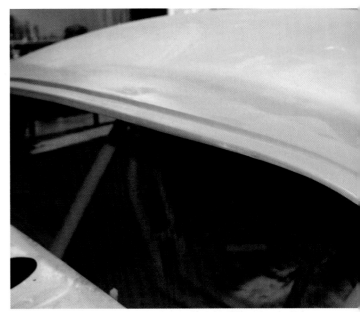

Now is the time to lay down a good coat of primer, filling the small spots and pinholes in the filler.

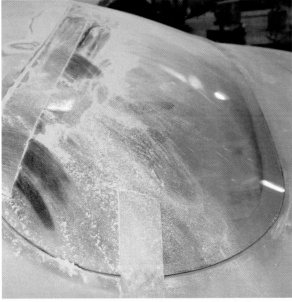

The window is once again added so the inner seal can be inspected. It is taped down for safety, as you do not want it falling out at this stage.

The rear window came out very well and looks great after the glass was installed and the car painted.

Next, we mixed up a large portion of Z-Grip filler on a pallet and proceeded to apply the filler between the window and the existing portion of the channel that we fabricated. You'll need some working time here, so don't over-catalyze the mixture or it will harden before you bed the glass. Use a rubber squeegee to work the filler between the glass and the existing metal so that the gaps are completely filled. You will be working from the inside of the car, and it may take more than one application of filler to fill in the spaces around the entire window.

Once we worked our way around the window, the filler was allowed to set up. You can check this by touching a spot of excess filler periodically. The best time to remove the glass from the bed is when the filler reaches a semi-hard,

rubbery state. If the filler is too soft, it may pull away from the metal. If it sets up completely, the glass will become lodged in place even with the wrapping.

Now all that's left is to remove the glass, peel off the protective cellophane, and make a final check for fit in the new bed. If there are any low spots or gaps between the glass and the bed, the filler procedure must be repeated in those spots. If the fit is good, the window can be set aside and the new window bed can be sanded and prepped for painting.

Appendix I

Manufacturer Source Guide

3M Company (abrasives, paint prep and metal treatment)
Web site: www.3M.com

Bend-Pak Incorporated (automotive lifts)
1645 Lemonwood Drive
Santa Paula, CA 93060
Local phone: (805) 933-9970, toll-free phone: 800-253-2363
Web site: www.bendpak.com

Bosch Tool Corporation (electric sheet metal shears, nibblers)
Web site: www.boschtools.com

Devilbiss Automotive Refinishing (painting equipment, spray guns, air regulators and filters)
Toll-free phone: 800-445-3988
Web site: www.autorefinishdevilbiss.com

Eagle Bending Machines
Phone: (251) 937-0947
Web site: www.eaglebendingmachines.com

Eastwood (restoration, autobody and metal-working tools)
263 Shoemaker Road
Pottstown, PA 19464
Toll-free phone: 800-345-1178
Web site: www.eastwood.com

E. P. Industries, Inc. (metal fabrication tools)
2305 Utah Avenue
El Segundo, CA 90245
Phone: (310) 245-8515
Web site: www.epindustries.com

ESAB (welding equipment and consumables)
Web site: www.esab.com

Evercoat (body fillers, primers, metal treatment, fiberglass materials)
6600 Cornell Road
Cincinnati, OH 45242
Phone: (513) 489-7600
Web site: www.evercoat.com

HammerHead (stainless-steel tool storage cabinets)
1400 N. Johnson Avenue, Suite 105
El Cajon, CA 92020
Phone: 800-261-0761
Web site: www.hammerheadsteel.com

House of Kolor (custom automotive paint)
210 Crosby Street
Picayune, Mississippi 39466
Phone: (601) 798-4229
Web site: www.houseofkolor.com

Lincoln Electric Company (welding equipment)
22801 St. Clair Avenue
Cleveland, OH 44117
Phone: (216) 481-8100
Web site: www.lincolnelectric.com

M&K Metal Company (metal supplier)
14108 So. Western Avenue
Gardena, CA 90249
Phone: (310) 327-9011

Mac Tools (automotive tools and tool storage)
Web site: www.mactools.com

Milwaukee Electric Tool Corporation (electric sheet metal shears and nibblers)
13135 W. Lisbon Road
Brookfield, WI 53005
Toll-free phone: 800-729-3878
Web site: www.milwaukeetool.com

Motor Guard Corporation (Magna Spot welders)
580 Carnegie Street
Manteca, CA 95337
Phone: (209) 239-9191
Web site: www.motorguard.com

Napa Auto Parts (auto parts, tools and hardware)
Web site: www.napaonline.com

National Detroit, Inc. (pneumatic sanding, grinding and
    buffing tools)
P.O. Box 2285
Rockford, IL 61131
Phone: (815) 877-4041
Web site: www.nationaldetroit.com

Special Effect Supply Corp. (vacuum-forming machines)
164 East Center Street
North Salt Lake, UT 84054
Phone: (801) 936-9762
Web site: www.fxsupply.com

Sata (automotive painting equipment)
Web site: www.sata.com/usa/

Snap-On Tools (automotive tools and tool storage)
Web site: www.snapon.com

Tools USA—Standard Tools and Equipment (automotive
    spray booths, automotive tools)
4810 Clover Road
Greensboro, NC 27405
Toll-free phone: 800-451-2425
Web site: www.toolsusa.com

Appendix II

Glossary— Customizer's Words, Terms, Acronyms and Definitions

A

ABRASIVE WHEEL: A metal-grinding or cutting wheel composed of abrasive grits and a bonding agent to hold the grit together.

ACCELERATOR: Additive to paint to speed the cure of a coating. An additive to polyester resin that reacts with catalyst to speed up polymerization. This additive is required in room temperature-cured resins. See promoter.

ACETONE: A ketone group solvent used to dissolve polyester resins. Used to a large extent for clean up of tools in fiberglass operations.

ACRYLIC: A plastic produced from acrylic acid or a derivative. Material used in the manufacturing of paint to increase gloss and durability.

ADDITIVE: A chemical added to a paint to improve or create certain specific characteristics. Any number of materials used to modify the properties of polymer resins. Categories of additives include reagents, fillers, viscosity modifiers, pigments and others.

ADHESION PROMOTER: Material used over an O.E.M. or cured insoluble finish to increase the adhesion of the topcoat.

AIR DRY: The evaporation of solvent in an undercoat or topcoat at room temperature.

AK STEEL: Aluminum-killed steel treated with a strong deoxidizing agent, in this case, aluminum, to reduce oxygen content, which prevents the forming of pinholes as the steel solidifies. AK steel has a fine-grain structure and is more stable at high temperatures than non-treated steel.

ALLOY: Metal composed of two or more elements to produce a desired quality in the metal.

ALLOY STEEL: Carbon steel with one or more elements added to produce a desired quality.

ALUMINUM PIGMENT: Small aluminum particles used in paint to reflect light. These flakes vary in size and polish to give a look of glamour and luster.

ANNEALING: Heating metal to a specific temperature followed by controlled cooling to produce a desired quality. Usually to induce softness.

ANSI: American National Standards Institute

ARC WELDING: A welding process using heat produced by an electric arc.

ARCING (the gun): The action of turning the wrist or elbow at the end of each pass of paint while doing blends or panel repair. This causes a lighter application of paint at each end of the pattern.

ASPECT RATIO: The ratio of length to diameter of a fiber.

ASTM: American Society for Testing and Materials

ATOMIZE: The breaking-up of paint into fine particles or droplets by a paint gun.

B

BAKING: The process of applying heat to a finish to speed the cure or dry time of the finish.

BARE SUBSTRATE: Any material (steel, aluminum, plastic, etc.) that does not have a coating of paint or primer.

BASECOAT: A highly pigmented color that requires a coating of clear for protection, durability and gloss.

BASECOAT/CLEARCOAT SYSTEM: A two-stage finish consisting of a base color coat and a clear top coat.

BI-DIRECTIONAL: Reinforcing fibers that are arranged in two directions, usually at right angles to each other.

BINDER: A resin-soluble adhesive that secures the random fibers in chopped strand mat or continuous strand roving.

BLEEDING: Soluble dyes or pigments in old finishes dissolved by solvents in new color that bleed through to the new finish color.

BLENDING: The tapering of finishes or colors so slight

differences cannot be distinguished. Merging one color into another. This is achieved by allowing some of the old finish to show through the new color.

BLISTERING: Effect of pressure from either solvent or moisture under a coating causing a swelling or blister in the finish; i.e. water blister. A flaw either between layers of laminate or between the gel coat film and laminate.

BLUSHING: A milky appearance of a topcoat that occurs when high humidity is present in the painting environment. When a fast-drying paint such as lacquer is applied, water condenses on or in the wet coating. This can be eliminated by use of heat or a slower solvent or retarder.

BODY FILLER: A moldable catalyst-activated polyester-based plastic material used on bare substrate to fill dents in damaged auto body parts.

BOND STRENGTH: The amount of adhesion between bonded surfaces; a measure of the stress required to separate a layer of material from the base to which it is bonded.

BRAZE WELDING: A welding process in which the filler metal has a melting point below that of the base metal.

BRIDGING: Occurrence where a primer or surfacer does not totally fill a sandscratch or imperfection. Not usually apparent in undercoat, however, does show up in topcoat.

BRITTLE: A paint coating lacking flexibility.

BUBBLES: Air or solvent trapped in a paint film caused by poor atomization during spraying. Air trapped in body filler caused by excessive agitation.

BUFFING/COMPOUNDING: Using a mild abrasive to bring out gloss and/or remove texture in a topcoat. This can be done by hand or machine.

BURN/BURN THROUGH: Polishing or buffing of a color or clear too hard or long causing the underlying coat(s) to be revealed.

C

CASE HARDENING: A heat-treating process that alters the surface layer of metal to increase its hardness over the core metal.

CASTING: The process of pouring a mixture of resin, fillers and/or fibers into a mold as opposed to building up layers through lamination. This technique produces physical properties different from laminating.

CATALYST: Technically considered an initiator. The name given to the chemical added to resin or gel coat to initiate cure. Additive for paint to enhance the curing process.

CELLULOSE: Natural polymer or resin derived from cottonseed oil to make paint coatings.

CHALKING: The result of weathering of a paint film resulting in a white powdery appearance.

CHANNEL: Is the lowering of a car over the frame by rising the section of the floor that the frame sits on. This requires a whole new floor board in most cases and makes a rusty car a perfect candidate for this process in many cases.

CHECKING: Sometimes called crow's feet. Tiny cracks or splitting in the surface of a paint film usually seen in a lacquer. Caused by improper film formation or excessive film build.

CHEMICAL STAIN/SPOTTING: Circular, oblong or irregular spots or discoloration on areas of finish caused by reactive chemicals coming into contact with air pollution (coal and high sulfur emissions), acid rain and snow.

CHIPPING: Removal of finish usually due to the impact of rocks and stones.

CHOP: Reducing the height of the top of a car by "chopping" out a section of material from a horizontal section of the roof near the window area.

CHOPPED STRAND MAT: A fiberglass reinforcement consisting of short strands of fiber arranged in a random pattern and held together with a binder.

COAT/SINGLE: Applying of undercoat or topcoat over the surface using a 50 percent overlap of spray.

COAT/DOUBLE: Two single coats with longer flash time.

COLORANT: Made with ground pigments, solvent and resin. Used in the intermix system to produce colors.

COLOR COAT: The application of color to a prepared surface.

COLOR MATCH: Two separate applications of paint exhibiting no perceptible difference in color shade or tone when viewed under the same conditions.

COLOR RETENTION: The ability of a color to retain its true shade over an extended period of time. A color that is color fast.

COLOR STANDARD: A small sprayed-out sample of OEM color. This is the established requirement for a given color code. This is the color the car is supposed to be from the factory.

COLOR VERSION: A color matched in a different quality finish, to match the same OEM standard; i.e., a color matched to an acrylic enamel in lacquer.

COMPLEMENTARY COLORS: Colors that are opposite each other on the color wheel.

COMPRESSIVE STRENGTH: The stress a given material can withstand when compressed. Described in ASTM D-695.

CONCENTRATION: The ratio of pigment in paint to resins in paint.

COVERAGE: The ability of a pigmented color to conceal or cover a surface.

CRATERING: The forming of holes in a film due to contamination.

CRAZING: Fine line cracks in the surface of the paint finish. Cracking of gel coat or resin due to stress.

CROSSCOAT: Applying paint in a crisscross pattern. Single coat applied in one direction with a second single coat applied at 90 degrees to the first.

CROW'S FEET: See Checking.

CURE: The chemical reaction of a coating during the drying process, leaving it insoluble.

CURDLING: The gelling or partial cure of paint due to incompatible materials.

CURTAINS: Large sagging or runs of paint due to improper application.

CUT IN: Painting of the edges of parts before installation.

CURE TIME: Time between introduction of catalyst or initiator to a polymer and final cure.

CURING AGENT: A catalytic or reactive agent which, when added to a resin, causes polymerization; synonymous with hardener.

CYCLE: The complete, repeating sequence of operations in a process or part of a process. In molding, the cycle time is the period (or elapsed time) between a certain point in one cycle and the same point in the next.

D

DEFINED ORIENTATION: The dispersion of metallic or mica flake with a definite pattern.

DELAMINATION: The peeling of a finish having improper adhesion. The separation of composite layers from each other.

DENSITY: A comparison of weight per volume, measured in pounds per cubic foot.

DEPTH: Lighter or darker in comparing two colors. The first adjustment in color matching.

DIE-BACK: The gradual loss of gloss due to continued evaporation of solvent after polishing.

DIRECT (FACE): The color viewed from head-on (90 degrees).

DISPERSION LACQUER: Particles of lacquer paint suspended or dispersed in a solvent that is not strong enough for total solution.

DISTORTION: A change in shape from that which is intended.

D.O.I. (DISTINCTNESS OF IMAGE): How clear a finish reflects an image.

DOUBLE COAT: A single coat of paint followed immediately by another.

DRAFT: The angle of the vertical components of a mold that allow removal of the part.

DRIER: A material used in a paint that enables it to cure.

DRY FILM THICKNESS (D.F.T.): The thickness of a paint after it has dried and/or cured. Measured in mils.

DRY SPOT: Area of incomplete surface film on laminated plastics; in laminated glass, an area over which the interlayer and the glass have not become bonded.

DRY SPRAY: The process of applying paint in a lighter, or not as wet, application.

E

ELASTIC LIMIT: The greatest stress that a material is capable of sustaining without permanent strain remaining upon the complete release of the stress. A material is said to have passed its elastic limit when the load is sufficient to initiate plastic, or non-recoverable, deformation.

ELECTROSTATIC PAINT APPLICATION: Process of applying paint by having the surface electrically charged positive or negative and the application equipment on opposite electric charge.

ELONGATION: Standard measure for the amount a sample can stretch as a percentage of original length before it fails or breaks.

ETCH: The process of chemically treating a material with an acid for corrosion resistance and adhesion of a primer, or to remove rust.

ETCHING PRIMER: A primer which contains an acid that etches the substrate as well as applying a primer. To protect against corrosion.

F

FACTORY PACKAGE COLOR (F.P.C.): Car colors that are matched, produced and packaged by paint manufacturers for specific car color codes for use at the refinish level.

FADING: A gradual change of color or gloss in a finish.

FATIGUE: The failure or decay of mechanical properties after repeated applications of stress.

FATIGUE LIFE: The number of cycles of deformation required to bring about failure of the test specimen under a given set of oscillating conditions.

FATIGUE LIMIT: The stress below which a material can be stressed cyclically for an infinite number of times without failure.

FATIGUE STRENGTH: The maximum cyclic stress a material can withstand for a given number of cycles before failure occurs; the residual strength after being subjected to fatigue.

FEATHEREDGE: A sanding process of tapering a broken paint edge to a smooth finish.

FEATHERING: Slang term for blending or slowly moving the edge of one color into a second color.

FEMALE MOLD: A concave mold used to precisely define the convex surface of a molded part.

FIBER ORIENTATION: Fiber alignment in a non-woven or a mat laminate where the majority of fibers are in the same direction, resulting in a higher strength in that direction.

FIBERGLASS: Glass that has been extruded into extremely fine filaments. These filaments vary in diameter, and are measured in microns. Glass filaments are treated with special binders and processed similar to textile fibers. These fibers come in many forms, such as roving, woven roving, mat and continuous strands.

FIBERGLASS CLOTH: A fiberglass reinforcement made by weaving strands of glass fiber yarns. Cloth is available in various weights measured in ounces per square yard or kg/m2.

FILLER: Usually an inert material added to plastic, resin or gel coat to vary the property, extend volume, or lower the cost of the article being produced.

FILLET: A rounded filing of the internal angle between two surfaces of a plastic molding.

FILM BUILD: The wet or dry thickness of applied coating

measured in mils (also see DRY FILM THICKNESS).

FISH EYE: The effect of surface contamination that causes a circular separation of a paint or gel coat.

FIXTURE: a tool or device used to position and hold a part during forming or fabrication.

FLAKE-OFF: Large pieces of paint or undercoat falling off of substrate; also called delamination.

FLANGE: An extension around the perimeter of a mold or part for the purpose of demolding, stiffening or connecting two components.

FLASH TIME: The time needed to allow solvents to evaporate from a freshly painted surface before applying another coat or heat.

FLATTENING AGENT: Material used in paint to dull or eliminate gloss.

FLEX AGENT: Material added to paint for additional flexibility, usually used for rubber or plastic flexible parts.

FLOATING: Characteristics or some pigments to separate from solution and migrate to the surface of paint film while still wet.

FLOP (SIDE TONE): The color of a finish when viewed from a side angle, other than direct.

FLOW: The leveling properties of a wet paint film.

FOGCOAT: A final atomized coat of paint, usually applied at higher air pressure and at greater distance than normal to aid in distributing the metallic particles of paint into an even pattern.

FOAM-IN-PLACE: The process of creating a foam by the combination of two liquid polymers.

FORCE DRY: Speed of dry due to application of heat.

G

GEL: The irreversible point at which a polymer changes from a liquid to a semi-solid. Sometimes called the "B" stage.

GEL COAT: A surface coat of a specialized polyester resin, either colored or clear, providing a cosmetic enhancement and weatherability to a fiberglass laminate.

GEL TIME: The length of time from catalyzation to gel or "B" stage.

GLAZE: A very fine polishing material used to gain gloss and shine.

GLOSS: Reflectance of light from a painted surface. Measured at different degrees by gloss meters.

GOOD SIDE: The side of a molding in contact with a mold surface.

GREEN: Resin that has not completely cured and is still rather soft and rubbery.

GRAYNESS: The amount of black or white in a specific color.

GRINDING: Operation using a coarse abrasive, usually a spinning disc to remove material such as metal, paint, undercoat, rust, etc.

GROUND COAT: Highly pigmented coat of paint applied before a transparent color to speed hiding.

GUIDE COAT: A mist coat of a different color, usually primer, to aid in getting a panel sanded straight. A dry contrasting color applied to prime prior to sanding. This coat remains in the low areas and imperfections during the sanding process. When removed, imperfections are eliminated.

GUIDE PIN: A pin which guides mold halves into alignment on closing.

H

HAND LAMINATE: The process of manually building up layers of fiberglass and resin using hand rollers, brushes and spray equipment.

HANDSLICK: The time it takes for a wet paint film to become ready for another coat of paint.

HARDENER: A substance or mixture added to a plastic composition to promote or control the curing action.

HARDNESS: Resistance to surface damage.

HEAT SINK: A material that absorbs or transfers heat away from a part.

HIGH BAKE: Baking a paint above 180 degrees F.

HIGH SOLID: Paints and undercoats that have a higher percentage of pigment and resin (film formers).

HIGH STRENGTH/HIGH CONCENTRATED: The amount of pigment in the volume solid portion is in a higher amount, more pigment vs. resin.

HIGH VOLUME LOW PRESSURE (HVLP): Spray equipment that delivers material at a low pressure of no more than 10 psi (at the air cap), however, with greater volume of atomized material.

HIT: Small increment. A gradual increase in quantity. Term used in color adjustment.

HOLD-OUT (COLOR): The ability of an undercoat to stop or greatly reduce the topcoat from soaking into it.

HUMIDITY: The amount or degree of water vapor, or moisture, in the air measured in percent.

HYDRAULIC PRESS: A press in which the molding force is created by the pressure exerted on a fluid.

HYGROSCOPIC: Capable of absorbing and retaining atmospheric moisture.

I

IMPACT STRENGTH: The ability of a material to withstand shock loading; the work done in fracturing a test specimen in a specified manner under shock loading.

IMPREGNATE: To saturate with resin. The most common application is saturating fiberglass with a catalyzed resin.

INCANDESCENT LIGHT: Light emitted from a burning filament in a glass bulb.

INCREMENT: A gradual increase in quantity.

INFRARED LIGHT: Portion of electromagnetic spectrum just below the visible light range. Can be used to cure paint due to the heat produced.

INNERCOAT ADHESION: The ability of one coat of paint to stick to another coat.

INTERMIX: The mixing of specific colors by adding different components or colorants to produce a usable mixture at the paint store or shop level.

ISOCYANATE/POLYISOCYANATE: Toxic chemical material containing a functional group of nitrogen, carbon and oxygen, used in urethane catalyst and hardener to cross link material into a solid urethane film.

J

JACKSTRAWING: A visual effect of glass fiber turning white in a cured laminate. This usually does not affect the strength of a laminate, but could be an indication of material incompatibility.

JIG: Any fixture for holding parts in position while joining them together; also refers to a fixture that helps parts maintain their shape.

JOINT: A line or distinction formed when two panels are connected. Also referred to as a seam.

L

LACQUER: A type of paint that dries by solvent evaporation.

LAMINANT: The product of lamination. A composite consisting of a layer or layers of thermoset polymer and fiber reinforcement.

LAMINATE: To place into a mold a series of layers of polymer and reinforcement. The process of applying materials to a mold. To lay up.

LAMINATION: Applying a layer of glass and/or resin to a mold. Also used to describe a single ply of laminate.

LASER: Actually an acronym for light amplification by stimulated emission of radiation.

LAY: In glass fiber, the spacing of the roving bands on the roving package expressed in the number of bands per inch; in filament winding, the orientation of the ribbon with some reference, usually the axis of rotation.

LAYER: A single ply of lay up or laminate.

LAY UP: The act of building up successive layers of polymer and reinforcement. Layers of catalyzed resin and fiberglass or other reinforcements are applied to a mold in order to make a part.

LET DOWN: The process of reducing the intensity of a colorant or mass tone through the addition of white or silver, allowing you to see cast and strength.

LIFTING: The soaking of a solvent into a soluble undercoat causing swelling, then causing the topcoat to wrinkle from underneath.

LOW-BAKE: Baking of a paint film up to 180 degrees F.

LOW-PRESSURE COAT: The process of applying the final coat of paint at a lower air pressure. Used to uniform a finish or blending.

M

MALE MOLD: A convex mold where the concave surface of the part is precisely defined by the mold surface.

MASKING: Using tape and paper to prevent paint from being applied where it is not wanted.

MASSTONE: The color of an undiluted colorant.

MASTER (PLUG): A full-scale representation of the intended part, usually retained as a reference and the part from which production molds are made.

METHYL ETHYL KETONE: Solvent used in many paint reducers and thinners.

METALLIC COLOR: Colors containing various sizes of aluminum flakes. These flakes have reflective properties and, when used in combinations and/or amounts, modify the optical characteristics of the color.

METAMERISM: A phenomenon exhibited by two colors that match under one or more light sources, but do not match under all light sources or viewing conditions.

MICA COLOR: Colors containing various sizes and/or colors of mica. Mica flakes have several optical characteristics allowing light to reflect, pass through and absorb. When added to color alone or with metallic flake, it causes the color to look different depending on the angle of view.

MIG: metal inert gas

MIL: Relative to paint, it refers to film thickness as a measurement equal to one-thousandth of an inch, or .0254 millimeter. A typical factory-type paint consisting of an undercoat and topcoat should measure approximately 8 mils.

"MINI BELL": Equipment used to apply paint electrostatically consisting of a spinning disk to which paint is applied. The spinning disc is charged electrically and paint is atomized through centrifugal force.

MIST COAT: A thin coat sprayed to uniform metallic finishes. Also used to blend colors. Sometimes used with light amounts of solvents to uniform finish and/or increase gloss.

MOTTLING: Blotches of metallic or mica particles in a paint film.

MICROBALLOONS: Microscopic bubbles of glass, ceramic or phenolic, used as a filler or to create syntactic foam or putty mixtures.

MICRON: One micron = .001 millimeter = .00003937 inch.

MODULUS OF ELASTICITY: An engineering term used to describe a material's ability to bend without losing its ability to return to its original physical properties.

MOLD: The tool used to fabricate the desired part shape. Also used to describe the process of making a part in a mold.

MOLDING: The process of using a mold to form a part.

MOLD RELEASE: A wax or polymer compound that is applied to the mold surface and acts as a barrier between the mold and the part, thus preventing the part from bonding to the mold.

MOLD SHRINKAGE: The immediate shrinkage which a molded part undergoes when it is removed from a mold and cooled to room temperature; the difference in dimensions, expressed in inches per inch between a molding and the mold cavity in which it was molded (at normal temperature measurement); the incremental difference between the dimensions of the molding and the mold from which it was made, expressed as a percentage of the dimensions of the mold.

M.S.D.S. (MATERIAL SAFETY DATA SHEETS): Contains information and specifications on a chemical or material. M.S.D.S. data on specific chemicals or materials can be obtained from their respective manufacturers.

N

NITRIDING: hardening process of adding nitrogen to the surface layer of steel.

NITROCELLULOSE: A type of lacquer paint. Also referred to as "straight" lacquer.

O

ORANGE PEEL: A gel coated or painted finish that is not smooth and is patterned similar to an orange's skin.

P

PARTING AGENT: See Mold Release

PARTING LINE: The location on a molded product between different segments of the mold used to produce the product.

PATTERN: The initial model for making fiberglass molds. See Plug.

PEENING: Working of metal by hammer blows or shot blasting to increase hardness.

PLASMA: A gas heated to a high temperature that becomes ionized, thereby able to penetrate through metal.

PLUG: A composite industry term for a pattern or model.

POT LIFE: The time during which the catalyzed resin remains liquid or "workable." See Gel Time.

PRIMER-SURFACER: A sandable undercoat formulated to fill minute surface imperfections in preparation for paint.

PUTTY: A thickened mixture of resin made by adding fillers, thixotrophs and reinforcing fibers.

R

RELEASE AGENT: A compound used to reduce surface tension or adhesion between a mold and a part.

RESIN: A liquid polymer that, when catalyzed, cures to a solid state.

S

SEALER: Material applied before topcoat to increase color holdout and uniformity of color and adhesion.

SEAM: See Joint.

SECONDARY COLORS: Mixture of two primary colors to produce a second color. Example: red and yellow make orange.

SEEDY: Rough or gritty appearance of paint due to very small insoluble particles.

SHEAR EDGE: The cut-off edge of the mold.

SHIP LAP: Method of joining two panels together with one panel having a recessed shelf to receive the other panel on top of it, leaving a flush surface.

SIDETONE "FLOP": The color of a finish when viewed from a side angle.

SINGLE STAGE: A one-step paint procedure of applying color, protection and durability in one application. No clear is used.

SIPHON FEED GUN: Any paint gun that uses air flowing over an opening to create a vacuum to draw paint up a tube to be atomized.

SLAG: Residual metal byproduct of welding processes.

S.M.C.: Sheet-molded compound, usually a polyester-based, fiberglass-reinforced material, such as panels of a Corvette body.

SOLIDS: The part of the paint, pigments and resin that do not evaporate.

SOLID COLOR: Colors that contain no metallic flakes in the pigment portion of paint. These colors have opaque pigmentation or properties in the paint film.

SOLUTION: A homogeneous mixture of two or more dissimilar substances.

SOLVENT CLEANER: Solvent-based cleaning material used to remove contamination from surfaces prior to refinishing.

SOLVENT POP: Blisters in the surface of a film caused by trapped solvent.

SPLITTING: The breaking open of an undercoat or topcoat into long cracks resembling the look of a dry river bottom.

SPOT REPAIR: The process of repairing only a portion of a panel or vehicle.

SPRAY PATTERN: Spray from the paint gun adjusted from a very small, almost round pattern to a wide, flat, somewhat oval shape.

STABILIZER: Special resin-containing solvent used in basecoat color to lower viscosity, helping in metallic control and recoat times.

STRENGTH OF COLOR: The hiding ability of a pigmented toner or colorant.

STIFFNESS: The relationship of load and deformation; a term often used when the relationship of stress to strain does not conform to the definition of Young's modulus.

STRESS-STRAIN CURVE: Simultaneous readings of load and deformation, converted to stress and strain, are plotted as ordinates and abscissas, respectively, to obtain a stress-strain diagram.

STRESS RELIEVING: Heating metal to a specific temperature and holding it until internal stresses are reduced. Slow cooling is required to prevent new residual stresses.

SYNTATIC FOAM: A foam made by mixing microspheres with a resin.

T

TACK: Surface stickiness.

TACK COAT: Usually the first light coat of paint that is allowed to set and become sticky before additional coats are applied.

TACK FREE: Time in the drying of a paint film where it is not sticky, but not completely cured.

TACK RAG: A sticky cheesecloth used to remove dust before painting.

TEMPERING: heating metal to a specific temperature followed by controlled cooling at a rate to reduce stress or to develop strength qualities.

TENSILE ELONGATION: An engineering term referring to the amount of stretch a sample experiences during tensile strain.

TENSILE LOAD: A pulling load applied to opposite ends of a given sample.

TENSILE STRENGTH: A measurement of the tensile load a sample can withstand.

THERMAL CONDUCTIVITY: Measures the transfer of heat through a material.

THERMOSPLASTIC PAINT: Material which becomes soft and pliable when heated, returning to solid when cooled, i.e., lacquer.

THERMOSETTING PAINT: Type of paint that becomes hard when heated and thereafter is cured; i.e., enamels, urethanes.

THINNER: Solvent material used to reduce the viscosity of lacquers.

THREE-STAGE SYSTEM: A three-step paint procedure involving a groundcoat, intermediate coat and transparent mica coat. This finish requires a clearcoat for gloss, protection and durability, which is applied last.

TIG: Tungsten inert gas

TINT: A pure toner used for the changing of another color.

TITANIUM DIOXIDE: A commonly used white pigment with high hiding quality.

TONERS: Made with ground pigments, solvent and resin. Used in the intermix system to produce colors.

TOP-COAT: The pigmented color portion of the painting process.

TRANSFER-EFFICIENCY: The ratio in a percentage of the amount of paint actually applied to a surface compared to the amount of material used.

TRANSLUCENT: Permits a percentage of light to pass but not optically clear like window glass.

TWO-COMPONENT: A paint material that must have a catalyst or hardener to react.

U

ULTRA VIOLET (UV) LIGHT: The part of the electromagnetic spectrum that can cause fading of paint. Located just beyond the visible part of spectrum.

UNDERCOAT: The coatings below the top color coat that help in adhesion and corrosion resistance.

ULTIMATE TENSILE STRENGTH: The ultimate or final stress sustained by a specimen in a tension test; the stress at moment of rupture.

UNDERCUT: An area of a part or mold that has an acute angle between two surfaces. If a part has an undercut a split mold is necessary.

UNIDIRECTIONAL: Strength lying mainly in one direction.

V

VISCOSITY: Measure of a fluid's quality of flow. Determined by allowing a measured amount to flow through an orifice and measuring the time it takes for this amount to flow.

VISCOSITY CUP: A tool used to meter the viscosity of paint to ensure precise reduction.

VIVAK: A thin high-impact plastic that is much cheaper than polycarbonate and can be drilled, cut and formed with heat for special projects. Vivak can be heat-formed at 280 to 320 degrees F. It can also be bonded by Vivak solvent to make three-dimensional shapes.

W

WATERBORNE COATING: A coating containing more than 5 percent water in its volatile fraction.

WAX: A compound used as a release agent. See Release Agent.

WORK HARDNESS: a condition resulting from cold-working of metal.